I0416848

AUDIT OF THE FEDERAL BUREAU OF INVESTIGATION'S AND THE NATIONAL SECURITY DIVISION'S EFFORTS TO COORDINATE AND ADDRESS TERRORIST FINANCING

EXECUTIVE SUMMARY

Our audit assessed programs implemented by the Federal Bureau of Investigation (FBI) and National Security Division (NSD) to identify, investigate, and prosecute terrorist financing. We found that the FBI and NSD have mechanisms to ensure terrorist financing-related information is shared and coordinated with each other and with other relevant law enforcement organizations and intelligence agencies. However, we found that the FBI could improve some case management practices associated with investigating terrorist financing.

In August 2005, the FBI Terrorist Financing Operations Section (TFOS) recommended that FBI field offices consider the use, where appropriate, of six basic financial-related investigative techniques when conducting counterterrorism investigations.[1] According to TFOS, these investigative techniques are: (1) FBI database inquiries, (2) FinCEN data inquiries, (3) government-wide database inquiries, (4) public and commercial database inquiries, (5) credit history checks, and (6) the identification and review of bank account activity.[2]

The FBI directed each field office to focus on financial information in counterterrorism cases and establish a financial investigative sub-file for all counterterrorism investigations. Also, each FBI field office was instructed to designate a Terrorist Financing Coordinator to serve as a liaison between the field offices and the Terrorist Financing Operations Section.

The case files we reviewed did not always contain documentation of the use of financial-related investigative techniques or for not using techniques when it appeared unnecessary to do so. According to the FBI, Special Agents are not required to document each action it deems unnecessary to take and doing so may be unduly burdensome and

---

[1] The term "strong consideration" was contained in an August 2005 electronic communication that directed the financial focus for all counterterrorism investigations.

[2] The Attorney General Guidelines for FBI Domestic Operations and the Domestic Investigations and Operations Guide call for the FBI to employ the least intrusive means that do not otherwise compromise FBI operations. Search warrants, wiretaps, and undercover operations are very intrusive. By contrast, investigative methods with limited procedural requirements, such as checks of government and commercial data bases and communication with established sources, are less intrusive.

inefficient. However, in our judgment better-supported case files enable succeeding Special Agents and FBI managers to determine whether a given counterterrorism investigation included an appropriate financial focus. In addition, clearly documenting the use of financial-related investigative techniques or valid reasons for not using these techniques is consistent with FBI investigative and case-file management requirements. FBI field offices are required to ensure that all reasonable investigative techniques have been exploited during each terrorism investigation. When closing such investigations, field office staff affirms that they have exhausted reasonable and practical intelligence collection methods and that investigative methods and techniques initiated have been completed or discontinued.

We determined that the FBI documented the use of or provided a valid reason for not using FBI database inquiries for 100 percent of the case files reviewed. For the remaining five techniques, we or the FBI identified documentation of the use of or valid reasons for not using the techniques in most but not all sampled cases.

The FBI issued a directive to focus on the financial aspects in counterterrorism cases by creating a specific sub-file for all counterterrorism investigations, but we found that Special Agents did not always adhere to this directive.

We also found that during the review period Terrorist Financing Coordinators did not routinely review counterterrorism cases to ensure the field offices implemented the financial focus directive for counterterrorism investigations. We believe it is important that all criminal and counterterrorism cases be reviewed for a potential nexus to terrorist financing so that FBI management can seek to achieve a consistent approach to applying financial-related investigative techniques. Our review found that the coordinators did not always perform their duties as intended by the FBI, performed unrelated collateral duties, and were not always selected in accordance with TFOS guidance.

The Department considers terrorist financing-related matters to be a subset of its counterterrorism investigations. Our audit found that the FBI and NSD share information and coordinate with federal, state, local, and international entities through programs and initiatives that address terrorism in its entirety and that include matters involving terrorist financing. We believe this approach is appropriate and provides better opportunities to dismantle and disrupt the entire structure of a terrorist organization.

We make eight recommendations to assist the FBI in appropriately identifying and investigating terrorism-related financing activities.

This report provides the full results of our review of the FBI's and NSD's implementation of programs to identify, investigate, and prosecute terrorist financing and both agencies' efforts to coordinate and share information to combat terrorist financing.

TABLE OF CONTENTS

INTRODUCTION

The Department of Justice's (Department) Strategic Plan identifies terrorism as our country's most significant national threat, and the plan's first goal is to "Prevent Terrorism and Promote National Security." In accordance with the strategic plan, the Department's first priority is to protect the United States against terrorism by preventing, disrupting, and defeating terrorist operations before they occur. As part of this effort, the Department works to identify, track, and dismantle financial structures that support terrorist groups.

Background

To operate, terrorist groups must have the resources to raise funds and the means to launder funds. Whether the funding is minimal or substantial, terrorist financing activities leave a financial trail that can be tracked.

Terrorist financing is referred to by American law enforcement as the act of knowingly providing something of value to persons or groups engaged in terrorist activity.[1] Terrorist groups move funds using the formal banking system; informal value-transfer systems; "Hawalas" or "Hundis"; and the physical smuggling of cash, gold, and other valuables.[2]

Terrorist financing may involve funds that, prior to remittance, are unconnected to any illegal activity.[3] Terrorist groups may obtain funds from seemingly legitimate sources such as business profits, donations, community solicitation, and other fundraising initiatives. Individuals involved with the funding source may not know the illegal end of the funds provided. A

---

[1] Since 1994, terrorist financing has been officially recognized as a crime with the enactment of the first material support statute, 18 U.S.C. § 2339A. Material support includes humanitarian aid, training, expert advice, or services in almost any form. Prior to 1994, terrorist financing could only be addressed through money laundering prosecutions.

[2] Informal value-transfer systems refers to any system, mechanism, or network of people that receive money for the purpose of making the funds or an equivalent value payable to a third party in another geographic location. Hawalas, which are sometimes referred to as Hundis, are a system of money transfer whereby customers entrust money to an individual who facilitates the money movement worldwide through personal connections or legitimate bank accounts with a minimal paper trail.

[3] Remittance involves the sending of money from one place to another.

common example of terrorist financing occurs when an individual donates funds to charities that serve as "fronts" for terrorist organizations.[4]

Terrorist groups may also obtain funds derived from criminal activities that include kidnapping, extortion, smuggling, and fraud. Terrorist groups use techniques similar to money laundering to evade authorities and to protect the identity of their sources and the beneficiaries of their funds. Financial transactions associated with terrorist financing tend to be in smaller amounts than those associated with money laundering.[5] Money laundering differs from terrorist financing in that it involves the act of turning "dirty" money into "clean" money. With money laundering, criminals conceal or disguise the nature, the location, the source, the ownership, or the control of the proceeds of specified unlawful activity.

Terrorist operations may be inexpensive and financing such operations is often covered by the larger financial resources allocated for the terrorist group's political and social activities, which makes it more difficult to uncover the illegal nexus. The September 2001 attacks on the United States cost about $500,000, according to the National Commission on Terrorist Attacks, and according to press reports, the 2010 plot to bomb Times Square cost less than $7,000.

Within the Department, the Federal Bureau of Investigation (FBI) takes the lead in conducting counterterrorism investigations, of which terrorist financing investigations are a subset. The National Security Division (NSD) takes the lead in coordinating national security investigations, including terrorist financing investigations. The *USA PATRIOT Improvement and Reauthorization Act* created the NSD in March 2006 to combat terrorism and other threats to national security through coordination and unity of purpose between prosecutors, law enforcement agencies, attorneys, and the intelligence community.[6]

---

[4] A front serves as a cover or disguise for some other activity, especially one of a secret or illegal nature.

[5] Money laundering is the conducting or attempt to conduct a financial transaction that involves the proceeds or property from some form of unlawful activity.

[6] The *USA PATRIOT Improvement and Reauthorization Act of 2005* (Act) made permanent most of the surveillance provisions of the 2001 USA PATRIOT Act. The Act also provided a 4-year extension of provisions granting roving surveillance authority under the *Foreign Intelligence Surveillance Act of 1978* and authorized the Director of the FBI to apply for a court order for the production of records for foreign intelligence and international terrorism investigations.

The FBI's Counterterrorism Organization

Terrorist financing enforcement is critical in the Department's efforts to address terrorism. Through its National Security Branch, the FBI addresses counterterrorism through intelligence and operations to support global counterterrorism activities. The National Security Branch's Counterterrorism Division (CTD) supports these objectives by, among other things, collecting, reporting, and analyzing critical information.[7] By combining intelligence and operations, the CTD seeks to mitigate threats and ensure an effective crisis response. The CTD consists of four branches, which are Operations I, Operations II, Analysis, and Operational Support. The Terrorist Financing Operations Section (TFOS) is a component of Operations Branch II.

After the attacks of September 11, 2001, the FBI and the Department identified a critical need for a more comprehensive and centralized approach to terrorist financial matters. Consequently, the FBI established an interagency Terrorism Financing Review Group (TFRG) to provide a comprehensive analysis of financial evidence obtained during the September 11 investigation and track the source and movement of funds within and outside the United States. Financial evidence established direct links among the hijackers and assisted in the identification of co-conspirators. Comprised of representatives from the Department, the FBI's Financial Crime and Counterterrorism Divisions, the Internal Revenue Service's Criminal Investigation Division, the U.S. Customs Service, the Department of the Treasury's Financial Crimes Enforcement Network (FinCEN) and Office of Foreign Asset Control, U.S. Postal Inspection Service, U.S. Secret Service, and Inspector General community, the TFRG combined relevant databases, unique skills, and resources.[8]

The FBI restructured the TFRG, renamed it the Terrorist Financing Operations Section, and placed it within the CTD's Operations Branch II.[9] The mission of TFOS is to identify, investigate, disrupt, and dismantle all

---

[7] The CTD's mission is to prevent, disrupt, and defeat terrorist operations before they occur; to pursue the appropriate sanctions for those who have conducted, aided, and abetted those engaged in terrorist acts; and to provide crisis management following acts of terrorism against the United States and its interests.

[8] In March 2003, the U.S. Customs Service transferred to the Department of Homeland Security and became the U.S. Customs and Border Protection.

[9] Operations Branch I of the CTD supports, coordinates, and manages terrorist-related investigations through its two sections, which are the International Terrorism Operations Section (ITOS) I and ITOS II. ITOS staff members provide oversight of counterterrorism investigations within the continental United States (ITOS I) and in extraterritorial locations (ITOS II).

terrorist financial and fundraising activities. TFOS coordinates efforts to track and shut down terrorist financing and to exploit financing information in an effort to identify previously unknown terrorist cells and to recognize potential activity and planning. TFOS works to build on the FBI's expertise in conducting complex criminal financial investigations and long-established relationships with the financial service sector.

Through its headquarters-based staff, TFOS:

- conducts financial analysis of terrorist suspects and their financial support structures in the United States and abroad;

- coordinates joint participation, liaison, and outreach efforts to appropriately utilize financial information resources of private sector, government, and foreign entities;

- uses FBI and Legal Attaché expertise to exploit financial information from foreign law enforcement, including the overseas deployment of TFOS personnel;

- works jointly with the intelligence community to fully exploit intelligence to further terrorists' investigations;

- works jointly with prosecutors, law enforcement, and regulatory communities; and

- develops predictive models and conducts data analysis to identify previously unknown terrorist suspects.

At the time of the review, TFOS was organized into six units. In December 2010, the FBI reorganized TFOS so it could more effectively accomplish its mission by integrating strategic intelligence, developing processes to enhance counterterrorism investigations, and initiating operational program management for terrorist financing investigations.

The FBI's Efforts to Address Terrorist Financing

The FBI addresses terrorist financing through TFOS, national and international working groups, and coordination with other federal agencies such as the Departments of State and Defense. The Counterterrorism Division, along with TFOS, seeks to enhance the FBI's mission to address terrorist financing by providing directives and resources and by ensuring that appropriate consideration is given to the financial aspects of all counterterrorism investigations. Through TFOS, the FBI established programs and initiatives that directly involved the field offices and Special Agents in an effort to ensure that all counterterrorism investigations included a consideration of financial matters.

Terrorist Financing Coordinator Initiative

In April 2002, the FBI established the Terrorist Financing Coordinator (Coordinator) position in each field office, to serve as a liaison between field offices and TFOS. The FBI directed the field offices to use their Coordinators for assistance and provided guidance to the Coordinators to ensure that counterterrorism investigations included a financial component.

Mandatory Financial Investigative Sub-file

In August 2005, TFOS directed that field offices establish a financial focus for each preliminary and full counterterrorism investigation. To accomplish this, the FBI directed its field offices to establish a financial investigative sub-file within each counterterrorism case file that includes the financial-related investigative techniques used during these investigations.

At the same time, TFOS established six financial-related investigative techniques that should be given "strong consideration" when conducting all counterterrorism investigative matters.[10] According to TFOS, these investigative techniques are: (1) FBI database inquiries, (2) FinCEN data inquiries, (3) government-wide database inquiries, (4) public and commercial database inquiries, (5) credit history checks, and (6) the identification and review of bank account activity.

The NSD's Counterterrorism Organization

The NSD seeks to ensure that the national security-related activities of the United States are consistent with relevant law. The NSD also oversees terrorism investigations and prosecutions, handles counterespionage cases, obtains court authorization for the collection of foreign intelligence under the Foreign Intelligence Surveillance Act, and conducts oversight of intelligence agency compliance with certain national security legal requirements.[11]

---

[10] The term "strong consideration" was contained in the August 2005 electronic communication that directed the financial focus for all counterterrorism investigations.

[11] The *Foreign Intelligence Surveillance Act* established procedures for requesting judicial authorization for foreign intelligence surveillance and created the Foreign Intelligence Surveillance Court, 50 U.S.C. § 1801. The act was intended to increase the United States' counterintelligence separate from ordinary law enforcement surveillance.

The NSD's Counterterrorism Section provides assistance with investigations and prosecutions to prevent and disrupt terrorist acts. The Counterterrorism Section is the NSD's predominant entity for addressing terrorist financing. The Counterterrorism Section coordinates the Department's efforts to combat terrorist financing; collaborates with the FBI and the U.S. Attorney's Offices regarding its terrorism investigations; serves as co-counsel with and provides subject matter expertise and guidance to the U.S. Attorneys' Offices in terrorism prosecutions; reviews indictments, search warrants, and other types of process, and makes recommendations for authorization; works with international counterparts on terrorism investigations and prosecutions; and coordinates with state and local law enforcement.

The Counterespionage Section prosecutes and reviews cases that involve national security, coordinates cases that involve classified information of the federal government, and oversees the *Foreign Agents Registration Act*, which requires individuals and companies that act as foreign agents to make certain periodic disclosures.[12]

The Office of Intelligence serves as the federal government's representative before the Foreign Intelligence Surveillance Court and oversees the FBI and other agencies' national security activities to ensure adherence to the Constitution and federal law.

The Office of Law and Policy provides legal assistance and advice on national security law and policy; and oversees the development, coordination, and implementation of intelligence and national security within the Department. This office also serves as the Department's point of contact on national security policy to Congress and other federal agencies and assists Congress with developing national security legislation.

The Office of Justice for Victims of Overseas Terrorism conducts outreach to U.S. victims of international terrorism. This office monitors the investigation and prosecution of the perpetrators of overseas terrorist attacks, responds to congressional and citizen inquiries about the Department's efforts, and works with other Department agencies to ensure that the rights of victims and their families are respected.

---

[12] The *Foreign Agents Registration Act* requires persons acting as agents of foreign principals in a political or quasi-political capacity to make periodic public disclosure of their relationship with the foreign principal, as well as activities, receipts, and disbursements in support of those activities, 22 U.S.C § 611.

The NSD's Efforts to Address Terrorist Financing

The U.S. Attorneys' Offices and the NSD prosecute the crimes related to terrorist financing. The U.S. Attorneys' Offices must notify the NSD when initiating international terrorism investigations and obtain the NSD's approval before using certain investigative tools or bringing charges. The NSD coordinates with federal, state, and local agencies to provide advice and counsel on terrorism cases. It provides training, assists in the processing of Foreign Intelligence Surveillance Act warrants and other information collection tools, and oversees the production of court document requests that involve classified materials.

The NSD assists the Departments of State and the Treasury in designating individuals, groups, or entities as terrorists to freeze their assets or property to prevent the commission of future terrorist acts.

Prior Audits and Reviews

In November 2003, the Government Accountability Office (GAO) issued a report on terrorist financing that concluded U.S. agencies should systematically assess terrorists' use of alternative financing mechanisms.[13] The GAO review assessed the use of alternative financing mechanisms to earn, move, and store assets. The report stated that the FBI did not systematically collect and analyze data on alternative financing mechanisms. The report concluded that the lack of such data hindered the FBI from conducting systemic analysis of trends and patterns that focus on these mechanisms. Without such an assessment, the FBI did not have analyses that could aid in evaluating risk and prioritizing efforts.

In this report, the GAO recommended that the Director of the FBI, in consultation with relevant U.S. government agencies, systematically collect and analyze information involving terrorists' use of alternative financing mechanisms. In response to GAO's recommendation, the FBI published intelligence gathering requirements on its intranet website that included collection requirements for alternative financing mechanisms. As a direct response to GAO's recommendation, the FBI established the Program Management and Coordination Unit within TFOS.[14] In addition, the FBI's

---

[13] U.S. Government Accountability Office (GAO), *Terrorist Financing, U.S. Agencies Should Systematically Assess Terrorists' Use of Alternative Financing Mechanisms*, GAO-04-163 (November 2003).

[14] The Program Management and Coordination Unit serves as the administrative component of TFOS and is responsible for the management of the FBI's Terrorist Financing Coordinator Initiative.

Inspection Division revised its annual field office report to include terrorist financing-related issues.

In September 2009, the GAO submitted a report to Congress on the Department of the Treasury's efforts to combat illicit financing.[15] The Office of Terrorism and Financial Intelligence within the Department of the Treasury cited strong collaboration in information sharing between the Treasury's Financial Crimes Enforcement Network and the Department of Justice. However, the GAO found that officials of the Departments of Justice and State reported declining collaboration and unclear mechanisms to enhance or sustain the relationship. The Treasury's Office of Terrorism and Financial Intelligence stated in its response that they would redouble some of their current efforts and undertake some new efforts.

---

[15] U.S. GAO, *Combating Illicit Financing, Treasury's Office of Terrorism and Financial Intelligence Could Manage More Effectively to Achieve* GAO-09-794 (September 2009).

OIG FINDINGS AND RECOMMENDATIONS

I. THE FBI's IMPLEMENTATION OF PROGRAMS TO IDENTIFY, INVESTIGATE, AND PROSECUTE TERRORIST FINANCING ACTIVITIES

The FBI advised Special Agents to strongly consider the use of, where appropriate, financial-related techniques as a complement to other investigative techniques. In addition, to help provide a necessary degree of focus and organization to the investigation, the FBI required the creation of a financial-investigative sub-file for all counterterrorism cases. We evaluated these terrorist financing initiatives implemented by the FBI and found that the FBI could strengthen its terrorist financing program through improved case management practices. The case files we reviewed did not always contain documentation of the use of financial-related investigative techniques or for not using techniques when it appeared unnecessary to do so. We also found Special Agents did not always create the mandatory financial-investigative sub-file. Such documentation will help ensure case files can be reviewed for appropriate use of financial investigative techniques. In addition, better documented and organized case files provide FBI managers with the ability to evaluate their terrorist financing program and add value to the case management process when cases are reassigned or transferred. We also found that FBI field offices' Terrorist Financing Coordinators did not always assist Special Agents with the financial-related aspects of counterterrorism investigations as intended by the FBI.

Support for the Utilization of Terrorist Financing Techniques

In an August 2005 electronic communication to all FBI field offices, TFOS presented basic financial-related investigative techniques that should be given strong consideration, where appropriate, when conducting all counterterrorism investigative matters. These investigative techniques and their benefits are described in Exhibit 1.

Exhibit 1: Basic Financial Investigative Techniques for All Counterterrorism Investigative Matters

Financial-Related Investigative Techniques	Benefit
FBI Database Inquiries	The Investigative Data Warehouse allows users to query information from several databases, including classified systems such as the Automated Case Support system and the Universal Index, as well as unclassified systems. The Automated Case Support system maintains electronic copies of most documents in FBI case files and provides references to documents that exist in hardcopy only. This query also includes data from FinCEN and other government agency terrorism and non-terrorism related databases, which are also considered financial-related investigative techniques as shown below.
FinCEN Data Inquiries	This inquiry searches all Banking and Money-Laundering Suspicious Activity Reports (SAR) from the Department of the Treasury's FinCEN. Searching SAR can result in the immediate identification of subjects' addresses, businesses, associates, banks, bank account numbers, and potential criminal activity. SAR data can serve as a beginning to a financial investigation and provide valuable non-financial identifying data on a subject or entity of interest.
Government-Wide Database Inquiries	Databases maintained by local and state governments and agencies outside the Department can provide information such as business data, source of income, tax status, education, travel information, limited credit information, and telephone subscriber information.
Public and Commercial Database Inquiries	Civil and criminal court records pertaining to civil suits, settlements, divorce and legal separation and criminal actions may lead to the identification of hidden transactions or assets. These databases may also provide other sources of information available in public databases such as bankruptcy records, real estate records, probate and death records, tax assessor's records, and secretary of state records. Commercial databases can identify information concerning all property owned or leased, including associated persons who share mailing address.

Credit History Checks	Credit history checks may identify evidence of payments, previously undisclosed assets used to make payments on an account, third parties, principals, or co-conspirators who made payments on an account. Reviewing credit card purchases can establish a timeline of transactions to establish the travel patterns of subjects.
Review of Bank Account Activity	Bank records show account information, significant dates, locations of transactions, and the identity of the individuals and businesses involved. Deposits can reveal the source of funding, employment through payroll deposits, and wire transfers to and from foreign contacts, bank accounts, and domestic accounts. Automated teller machine transactions can reveal timelines of movement, nationally and internationally.

Source: TFOS Directive on Financial-Related Investigative Techniques

As shown in Exhibit 1, there are many benefits to employing these basic financial-related investigative techniques. According to *The Attorney General's Guidelines for FBI National Security Investigations*, the FBI has three levels of investigative activity in national security investigations: (1) threat assessments, (2) preliminary investigations, and (3) full investigations. All of these techniques are in accordance with authorized methods for each level of investigation.[16] Each level of a national security investigation can benefit from the prudent usage of financial-related investigative techniques.

In its August 2005 electronic communication to all field offices, the FBI advised that the usage, where appropriate, of financial-related investigative techniques can result in the identification of personal information, non-terrorism related criminal activity, previously unknown business and personal associations, travel patterns, communication methods, resource procurement, and Internet service providers. Special Agents can use these techniques to create historical timelines, which may be used to determine the location of an individual based on the geographic location of financial transactions, such as automated teller machine withdrawals. The FBI further

---

[16] The Attorney General Guidelines for FBI Domestic Operations and the Domestic Investigations and Operations Guide call for the FBI to employ the least intrusive means that do not otherwise compromise FBI operations. Search warrants, wiretaps, and undercover operations are very intrusive. By contrast, investigative methods with limited procedural requirements, such as checks of government and commercial data bases and communication with established sources, are less intrusive.

advised that these techniques often result in the development of additional leads and information that allow an agent to pursue more sophisticated investigative techniques. However, there are circumstances when these techniques cannot be applied during an investigation.[17]

We agree that the benefits obtained from use of the basic financial-related techniques is an important resource to the FBI's terrorist financing program. To assess how the FBI field offices addressed terrorist financing through the use of these techniques, we selected eight FBI field offices with the highest rate of counterterrorism activity. We reviewed a sample of counterterrorism investigations for documentation of the Special Agents' use of the six financial-related investigative techniques. Our review involved a two-step process. First, we reviewed case files to identify documentation of use of the techniques. We compiled the results of this review and presented those results to FBI managers. The FBI managers told us that they believed that field office staff used the techniques more extensively than our case file review indicated and endeavored to identify the support. The FBI managers identified additional support from various sources and we reviewed that support. The results of these reviews are summarized in Exhibit 2 and discussed below.

We reviewed 209 case files of which we selected 174 randomly and 35 judgmentally. We performed this review by evaluating the hard copy case files in eight field offices. We also discussed with Special Agents their use of the financial-related investigative techniques.

From our case file review, we found that the FBI field offices' files did not always include documentation for their use of financial-related investigative techniques. As shown in row 1 of Exhibit 2, we found that Special Agents provided documents for use of the FBI database inquiries, government-wide database checks, and public and commercial database checks in more than 60 percent of the 209 cases we reviewed. We identified documents for the Special Agents' use of FinCEN inquiry in only 13 percent, credit history in 29 percent, and bank activity in 35 percent of the files reviewed.

To obtain the additional support for use of financial-related investigative techniques, TFOS and FBI Inspection Division officials contacted Special Agents assigned to the sampled cases and reviewed the FBI's

---

[17] There are circumstances when a financial-related investigative technique may not be applicable. For example, this may occur when the case's subject is unidentifiable, a website or telephone number, or considered a non-U.S citizen. In such circumstances, the financial-related techniques may not be needed.

Automated Case Support system to obtain support for the use of the techniques. The FBI officials also provided additional details and explanations regarding cases in our sample for which not all financial-related investigative techniques were appropriate.

The FBI officials told us that some common reasons for techniques not being appropriate were: (1) the subject lived outside the United States, (2) the subject of the case was a website with no financial relations, (3) there was not a terrorism nexus, and (4) a subject was not identified. We agree that not all techniques were appropriate for all investigative circumstances. For example, when a subject lives outside the United States, there may be no need to review a credit history or conduct a review of bank account activity. Similarly, when the subject of an investigation is a website there may be no need to review FinCEN data or review a credit history.

We reviewed the additional documents provided by the FBI and agreed that for many sampled cases the documents demonstrated either use of the six financial-related investigative techniques or valid reasons for not using the techniques. Row 2 of Exhibit 2 summarizes the number of sample cases for which the FBI provided additional documents for the use of the techniques. Row 3 summarizes the number of sample cases for which the FBI supported valid reasons for not using the techniques. As shown in Row 4, the FBI documented that it used or did not need to use FBI database inquires for 100 percent of the cases we sampled. However, for the remaining five financial-related investigative techniques, the FBI did not document usage or provide reasons for not using the techniques in all of the sampled cases.

Exhibit 2: Support for the Special Agents Usage of the Financial-Related Investigative Techniques

		FBI Database Inquiry	FinCEN Gateway Inquiry	Government-wide Database Check	Public and Commercial Database Check	Credit History Check	Review Bank Account Activity
1	OIG's File Review	139 (67%)	27 (13%)	152 (73%)	142 (68%)	61 (29%)	74 (35%)
2	FBI's Additional Support and Explanations	62	128	40	39	13	18
3	Reasons Provided for Non-Usage	8	28	11	13	70	66
4	Sub-total	209 (100%)	183 (88%)	203 (97%)	194 (93%)	144 (69%)	158 (76%)
5	Support Not Provided	0	26	6	15	65	51
	Total	209	209	209	209	209	209

Source: OIG Analysis of Case Files and the FBI Research of Case Files

Regarding the items in Row 4, TFOS officials stated that the percentage of use for each technique in Row 4 reflected what they would expect given the FBI's practice of using the least intrusive techniques necessary to complete an investigation. For Row 5, FBI officials told us that to obtain documents for these items they would need to contact the original case agent and perform a full case file review in the field offices to determine how Special Agents documented their use of the financial-related investigative techniques. The officials said that such a review would allow them to assess the use of the technique or determine if there was a valid reason for not using the technique. They also said that reviewing an investigative case file is a very difficult task because each case involves a different range of both investigative activity and documentation for that activity. The officials said completion of such a review requires the work of Special Agents with years of training and experience. In part, the officials said, this is because many investigative techniques that may touch on financial-related matters are "inherent" to each investigation and may be documented in the case file separate from the financial investigative sub-file.

During our case file review, we reviewed the master file and sub files for relevant documents that documented the use of the financial-related investigative techniques. We understand and accept that documentation for use of the techniques may be located somewhere in the FBI's filing system, but we believe that documentation should be easily identified in the case files without the need for extensive searches performed by FBI officials or us. The documentation for a given technique's usage can be located in other sections of the case, for example, bank account activities may be located in the National Security Letter section of the case files. As discussed in the following section of this report, the FBI mandates a financial investigative sub-file to help ensure central documentation of financial investigative techniques. Such documentation in the sub-file would allow succeeding case agents, supervisors, and TFOS staff to assess financial investigative activity without the need for extensive searches of the case file. In addition, maintaining the files in this manner would ensure compliance with the Standards for Internal Control in the Federal Government that require all transactions and other significant events be clearly documented and that the documentation be readily available for examination.[18] FBI officials told us they disagree with the applicability of these standards to the management of investigative case files. However, we note that, per the Government Accountability Office, internal controls are synonymous with management controls and cover all aspects of an agency's operations (programmatic, financial, and compliance). As such, we believe the standards apply and add value to the FBI's case management practices.

Further, according to the FBI Domestic Investigations and Operations Guide, at the closing of a full investigation, field Special Agents must document whether all investigative methods or techniques initiated have been completed or discontinued. FBI field offices are required to ensure that all reasonable investigative techniques have been exploited during each terrorism investigation and must exhaust all reasonable and practical intelligence collection methods. In our judgment, better-supported case files would more clearly demonstrate the results of techniques used and explanations for not using a technique.

Cases Designated Specifically as Terrorist Financing Cases

In 2008, the FBI recognized the need for more accurate data relating to terrorist financing investigations, and TFOS developed new Criminal Problem Indicator (CPI) Codes that pertain specifically to terrorist financing issues in order to provide accurate information for congressional testimony and other initiatives regarding terrorist financing investigations. Of the 209 counterterrorism cases we sampled, Special Agents identified 57 as "terrorist financing" cases based on these codes.

---

[18] U.S. Government Accountability Office, *Standards for Internal Control in the Federal Government*, Report GAO/AIMD-00-21.3.1 (November 1999).

As shown in Exhibit 3, for terrorist financing cases, Special Agents applied the six financial-related investigative techniques about as often as for all the cases we sampled, and the FBI did not have support available for use of the techniques in all of the terrorist financing cases. Exhibit 2 relates to all counterterrorism cases and Exhibit 3 addresses cases that the FBI determined to be terrorist financing cases.

Exhibit 3: Support for the Special Agents Usage of Recommended Financial-Related Investigative Techniques for Terrorist Financing Cases

		FBI Database Inquiry	FinCEN Gateway Inquiry	Government-wide Database Check	Public and Commercial Database Check	Credit History Check	Review Bank Account Activity
1	OIG's File Review	37 (65%)	13 (23%)	46 (81%)	38 (67%)	19 (33%)	32 (56%)
2	FBI's Additional Support and Explanations	20	35	9	13	5	8
3	Reasons Provided for Non-Usage	0	2	0	2	16	11
4	Sub-total	57 (100%)	50 (88%)	55 (96%)	53 (93%)	40 (70%)	51 (89%)
5	Support Not Provided	0	7	2	4	17	6
	Total	57	57	57	57	57	57

Source: OIG Analysis of Case Files and the FBI Research of Case Files

Improvements Needed to Support the Use of Financial-Related Investigative Techniques

The FBI's Domestic Investigations and Operations Guide (DIOG) provides that each FBI component is responsible for creating and maintaining authentic, reliable, and trustworthy records. Such records:

- facilitate the documentation of official decisions, policies, activities, and transactions;

- facilitate the timely retrieval of needed information;

- ensure continuity of business;

- improve efficiency and productivity through effective records storage and retrieval methods;

16

- ensure compliance with applicable laws and regulations; and

- safeguard the FBI's mission-critical information.

During our file reviews in FBI field offices, we were unable to locate documents for the use of the six recommended financial-related investigative techniques for many of the sampled counterterrorism cases. FBI headquarters officials believed that additional documentation was available and, in an effort to locate such documents, they completed reviews of FBI data system records, e-mailed field office staff, and participated in discussions with field office staff. At the conclusion of this effort, the FBI located additional information and we agreed that documentation existed for either use of the techniques or appropriately not using the techniques in most of the sampled counterterrorism cases. However, as indicated in Exhibit 2, despite our file reviews and the FBI additional review efforts, complete documentation could not be located for five of the six techniques. FBI officials believe that additional documentation may be available elsewhere in the FBI files located in field offices.

Our initial fieldwork results showed the case files did not always include clear documentation of the use of the financial-related investigative techniques. The FBI expended a considerable amount of time and resources to support the Special Agents' use of the financial-related investigative techniques. Because of the need for these efforts, we believe the FBI could strengthen its terrorist financing program by ensuring Special Agents routinely document their usage of the financial-related investigative techniques for counterterrorism investigations. There should be clear documentation in the case files to document the use of the financial-related investigative techniques or a clear explanation of why the techniques were not appropriate for use.

In its 2005 electronic communication, TFOS also concluded that data obtained from field office surveys, Automated Case Support records, and numerous leads directed to TFOS showed that Special Agents often under-utilized basic financial-related investigative techniques. TFOS concluded that terrorism financing was often equated erroneously only with investigative matters that relate to terrorist fundraising. In the same communication, TFOS explained that a common misconception is that the application of financial-related investigative techniques is appropriate only in investigations involving entities and individuals suspected of raising funds in support of terrorism. TFOS officials believed, and we agree, that Special Agents should use financial-related investigative techniques in all counterterrorism investigations and not just those that involve terrorist fundraising.

In our judgment, with better-supported cases files supervisors can readily determine if the case agent used or properly considered the use of these techniques. Such documentation would enable field office supervisors and TFOS staff at FBI headquarters to ensure that appropriate financial-related investigative steps are taken in all counterterrorism investigations. When cases are transferred to another agent or office, complete support provides for efficient transition and ensures there is no duplication of work. The documented use of financial-related investigative techniques or explanations for not using the techniques allows the investigation to continue without delay. For these reasons, we believe that the FBI should enhance its process to ensure that case files include documented support regarding the use of financial-related investigative techniques.

Mandatory Financial Investigative Sub-file

To provide financial focus and organization to counterterrorism investigations, in August 2005 the FBI, sent an electronic communication to all field offices requiring the creation of a financial investigative sub-file. The sub-file was intended to provide financial focus and organization to counterterrorism investigations by ensuring that Special Agents give appropriate attention to the financial aspects of each preliminary and full counterterrorism investigation. The financial investigative sub-file was also intended to assist the Counterterrorism Division in carrying out its program management responsibilities. However, the August 2005 communication did not identify specific documents to be included in the sub-file.[19]

We reviewed the 209 sampled case files at the eight FBI field offices we visited to determine the extent to which Special Agents established financial investigative sub-files. We determined that for 76 percent of sampled case files (159 out of 209 cases) Special Agents opened the mandatory sub-file. For the remainder of the sampled cases, Special Agents

---

[19] At the time of our audit, the FBI had developed a draft Counterterrorism Policy Implementation Guide, which the FBI said it expected to finalize in the spring of 2011. The draft guide stated that field offices should use sub-files to organize intelligence information and maintain financial National Security Letters, financial records, and documents generated as a result of any financial analysis or intelligence collected on a subject's financial activities. National Security Letters give the FBI the power to obtain the disclosure of customer records held by banks, telephone companies, and Internet services providers.

did not open or had not yet opened the sub-file. Special Agents told us a sub-file was not used because some cases did not have a financial nexus, some of the subjects in other cases were not U.S. citizens, some Special Agents were not aware of the sub-file requirement, and in some cases financial investigative information was filed in a different sub-folder.

Although the Special Agents provided explanations for not creating a sub-file for their counterterrorism investigations, we believe the sub-file should be created because it can improve the case management process and provide a baseline for the financial focus. When a case is reassigned to another Special Agent, the sub-file also provides an overview of techniques performed by the previously assigned Special Agent. Without the sub-file, another Special Agent may not readily determine which techniques were used and it is difficult to tell whether Special Agents are adhering to the FBI's directive to enhance the financial aspects of its counterterrorism investigations. The FBI may not be able to determine whether Special Agents are giving appropriate attention to the financial aspects of each preliminary and full counterterrorism investigation. We believe the sub-file can be used as a central location for documenting the use of the financial-related investigative techniques or reasons for not using the techniques. When the documented support for the use of the financial-related techniques are centrally located, case file reviews are more efficient and staffing resources for these reviews are better utilized.

We interviewed 40 Special Agents (38 Special Agents and 2 Supervisory Special Agents) regarding their perceptions about whether the sub-file requirement encouraged them to use the recommended financial investigative tools. Eleven Special Agents told us they believed the use of the sub-file increased their focus on terrorist financing matters, but 24 said they did not believe that the sub-file led to such a focus.[20]

We also reviewed the documented support for the use and valid reasons for not using the financial-related investigative techniques to assess the Special Agents' use of the techniques when they opened sub-files and when they did not open sub-files for investigations. As shown in Exhibit 4, our results indicate that Special Agents employed these techniques at about the same rate when sub-files were opened as when they were not opened.

---

[20] Of the remaining five Special Agents we interviewed, two said they did not have knowledge of the sub-file and two were indifferent about the sub-file. We did not receive a response from one Special Agent.

Exhibit 4: Documented Usage of Financial-Related Investigative Techniques When Sub-files Were and Were Not Used

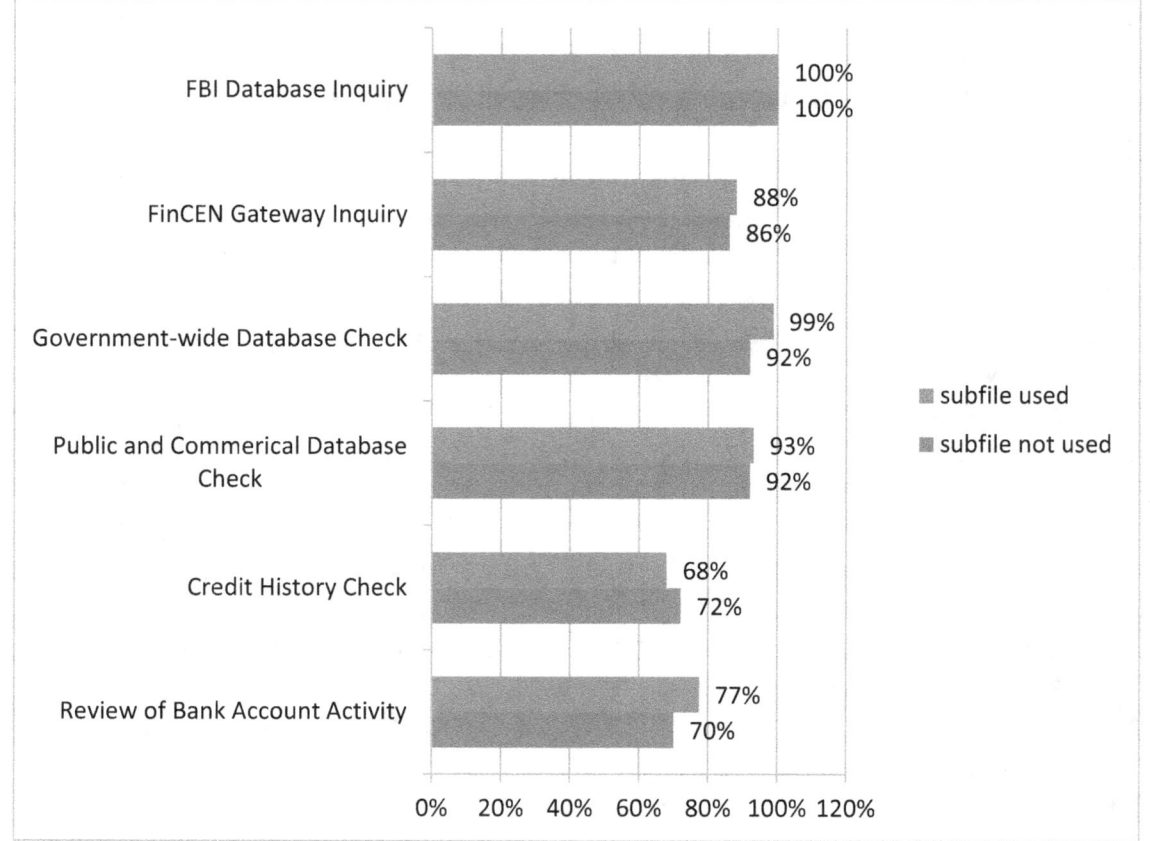

Source: OIG Review of FBI Case Files

Although these results show that the use of the sub-files may not have an impact on Special Agent's use of the six financial-related investigative techniques, we disagree with the 24 Special Agents who said they believe that the sub-file requirement does not encourage them to focus on using the recommended financial-related investigative techniques. In our judgment, the successful use of the sub-file by one-fourth of the Special Agents we interviewed demonstrates that full implementation of FBI management's decision to establish the sub-file can assist the Counterterrorism Division in carrying out its program management responsibilities by providing better oversight to ensure that field offices adhere to the mandatory financial focus requirement when conducting counterterrorism investigations. Further, when cases are transferred or reassigned, Special Agents can review the sub-file and easily determine whether any financial-related investigative techniques had been used during the investigation. We sought to identify areas of counterterrorism management that may affect the FBI's terrorist financing program.

Special Agents' Training and Background

At the eight field offices where we reviewed case files, we interviewed 40 Special Agents who worked on our sample cases and asked about the extent of their financial backgrounds and their training on financial-related investigative techniques. For purposes of our interviews, a financial background consisted of previous experience working in the financial industry. Similarly, ongoing financial training consisted of periodic training, to include trends in terrorist financing, offered by the Coordinator to field offices. Of the 40 Special Agents we interviewed, 30 did not have a financial background. Of these 30 Special Agents, 15 told us they had not received any training on financial-related investigative techniques.

The TFOS Section Chief told us that field Special Agents need additional training, and TFOS was planning a conference for Coordinators and Special Agents to reinforce the importance of the financial aspects of counterterrorism investigations.[21] Routine training would increase awareness of the benefits of the financial-related investigative techniques and improve the usage of these techniques.

Terrorist Financing Coordinator Position

We also reviewed the Terrorist Financing Coordinator position at the eight field offices we visited. Our results are discussed below.

In April 2002, the FBI requested field offices to designate a Terrorist Financing Coordinator to serve as a point of contact with the TFRG, which was subsequently renamed TFOS. Specific Coordinator duties include ensuring terrorist financing sub-files are active and contain financial investigative information. A March 2008 electronic communication expressed the importance of the Coordinator's role and directed field office staff to contact their coordinator with questions, assistance needs, and referrals to TFOS personnel.

To assess the FBI's implementation of the Terrorist Financing Coordinator initiative, we reviewed counterterrorism case files and interviewed Coordinators about their background and experience related to terrorist financing at eight FBI field offices. We also interviewed several TFOS officials at FBI headquarters about the Coordinator position.

---

[21] FBI designated Terrorist Financing Coordinators in each field office to assist with the implementation of the terrorist financing program.

Duties and Responsibilities

The March 2008 electronic communication specified that Coordinators:

- serve as the liaison between the field offices, Joint Terrorism Task Forces (JTTF), and TFOS;[22]

- attend all training conferences designated for Coordinators;

- participate in the Emergency Response Network to respond to queries that demand immediate resolution;

- assist in the coordination of the Terrorist Financing Coordinator national initiatives;

- review counterterrorism cases that have a potential terrorist financing component;

- identify criminal cases that may have a nexus to terrorist financing;

- engage in all counterterrorism investigations with a designated level of identification;

- serve as a liaison with the local banking community;

- articulate the investigative responsibilities and abilities of TFOS to the field office; and

- participate in domestic and international deployments.[23]

We believe Coordinators are not used as intended by the FBI to assist field Special Agents in the focus on terrorist financing matters. Exhibit 5 depicts how the eight Coordinators we interviewed described their duties. All Coordinators attended the annual training conferences and served as the liaison between the field offices and TFOS. Five of the eight Coordinators

---

[22] The JTTFs consist of FBI, state and local law enforcement officers and representatives of various federal agencies. The JTTFs are supervised by FBI Supervisory Special Agents and are managed locally by the Special Agents in Charge or Assistant Directors in Charge of the respective field offices. TFOS recommended Coordinators be assigned to field office JTTFs and partner with a financial specialist from other agencies.

[23] Coordinators can volunteer to be assigned to carry out terrorist financing investigations within or outside the United States.

served as a liaison with the local banking community. Three Coordinators performed the duties of identifying criminal cases with a nexus to terrorist financing and reviewing case files for a potential terrorist financing component. Only one Coordinator participated in domestic and international deployments and one assisted with the coordination of TFOS national initiatives.

Exhibit 5: Recommended Duties Performed by the Coordinators

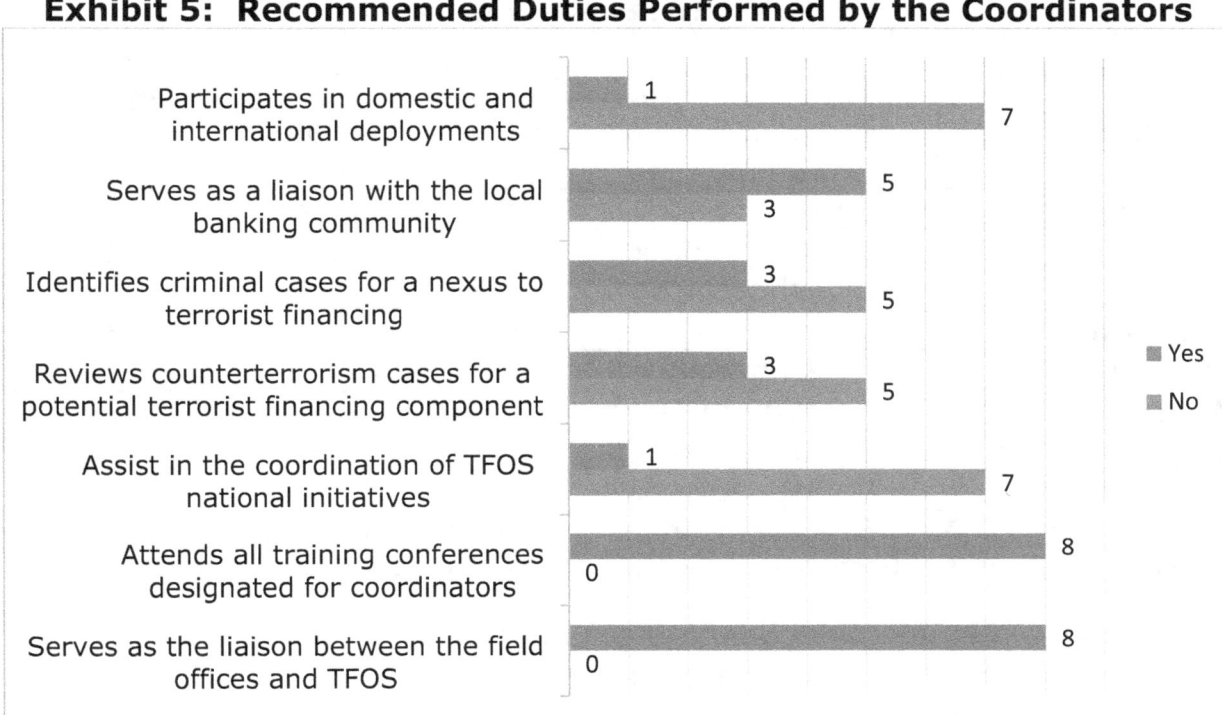

Source: OIG Analysis of Coordinator Duties

In addition, we compared Coordinators' work and the training they received to TFOS expectations. We focused on each Coordinator's: (1) background and selection, (2) extent of terrorist financing training received from TFOS, (3) technical assistance and training provided to the field offices, (4) review of counterterrorism and identification of criminal cases, and (5) involvement within the financial community.

Background and Selection of Coordinators

In March 2008, TFOS advised FBI field offices that each Coordinator should be a Special Agent with financial investigative experience. The communication did not provide details on the level of financial investigative experience required for the position. Of the eight Coordinators we interviewed, the FBI employed three as financial analysts and the remaining five were Special Agents. Five Coordinators (one financial analyst and four Special Agents) had a background in conducting investigations, one financial

23

analyst had a background in accounting and finance, and one Special Agent and one financial analyst had a background in financial crimes.[24] The Coordinators had between 3.5 and 23 years of experience with the FBI. Exhibit 6 summarizes the background, position, and years of experience with the FBI for these eight Coordinators.

Exhibit 6: Coordinator's Background and Experience at the Eight Field Offices We Visited

Location	Background	Position	Years of FBI Experience
Atlanta	Terrorist Financing Investigations	Financial Analyst	7
Chicago	Investigation	Special Agent	3.5
Detroit	Terrorist Financing Investigations	Special Agent	8
Houston	Financial Crimes	Financial Analyst	23
Los Angeles	Investigation	Special Agent	19
Miami	Accounting/Finance	Financial Analyst	11
New York City	Terrorist Financing Investigations	Special Agent	10
Washington, D.C.	Financial Crimes	Special Agent	9

Source: OIG Analysis of Coordinators' Background and Experience

Despite the recommendation that Coordinators should be Special Agents, 10 of the remaining 48 field offices designated a financial analyst or a forensic accountant as the Coordinator. During our audit, we learned that the FBI had not developed formal qualifications for the Coordinator position. TFOS officials told us they were aware that field offices selected financial analysts or forensic accountants as Coordinators. When we asked about general qualifications for a suitable candidate for the Coordinator position, TFOS officials told us that Special Agents were ideal candidates because they have experience investigating cases that a financial analyst would lack. In addition, a TFOS official told us that a Special Agent would have more credibility with other Special Agents to direct and advise investigative work. Nevertheless, TFOS officials told us that financial analysts often have more financial experience than Special Agents who are available for a Coordinator assignment. These officials told us it was not always practical to select a Special Agent designee, and that it was best to allow the field offices to choose the Coordinator designee.

---

[24] Of the five Coordinators with investigative experience, three had experience in terrorist financing investigations.

The March 2008 communication also stated that the Coordinator position was expected to be assigned on a full-time basis. However, the eight Coordinators we interviewed performed other duties in addition to those associated with their Coordinator roles. For the Special Agents, these general duties included planning and conducting investigations, collecting and evaluating information and intelligence, and providing advice and assistance to the U.S. Attorneys' Offices during prosecutions. The financial analysts' general duties consisted of examining, analyzing, extracting, and scheduling pertinent financial data from financial documents and identifying the types of financial documents and records needed to prove criminal allegations.

In May 2011, the FBI issued another electronic communication that officially modified the Coordinator's role and responsibilities. This communication stated that the selected Coordinator should be a qualified Special Agent or analyst with a successful track record for working counterterrorism investigations. It further stated the Coordinator should have a financial background; however, such a background was not mandated because, the communication stated, TFOS would provide financial training. Beyond stating that a Coordinator should be a qualified and experienced Special Agent or analyst, this communication did not establish specific qualifications for the Coordinator position.

Because resources and caseloads differ within each of the field offices, field offices cannot always select a Special Agent to be Coordinator as TFOS has recommended. As shown in Exhibit 6, the Coordinators we interviewed had different levels of experience. We believe the selection of the Coordinator should be based on field office resources and a potential candidate's skills and abilities, including financial investigative experience, so that selecting officials can make appropriate assessments of their staff. However, absent formally established qualifications for the Coordinator position, the potential exists for field offices to select a coordinator without the skills, abilities, or interest to perform the Coordinator's duties. In addition, without clearly defined expectations for the Coordinator position, the field offices may not receive the full benefit that Coordinators could provide.

Training Received and Provided

TFOS hosts a 3-day annual Terrorist Financing Conference that provides introductory training to new Coordinators and serves as refresher training to existing Coordinators. The annual conference consists of sessions and presentations that include: case study reviews, advanced financial investigative methods in terrorism cases, emerging trends in electronic money movement, information on sanctions and designations, intergovernmental and international assistance, information on financial crimes in terrorism cases, non-governmental organizations, and best practices. Attendance at the conference is mandatory for field office coordinators. Each of the Coordinators we interviewed attended the annual conference.

TFOS officials told us that it is the FBI's routine practice to survey conference participants to obtain feedback from the Coordinators about their experience and recommendations for future conferences. However, these officials were unable to locate the evaluation forms or any summary evaluation of those forms for the September 2010 conference. Consequently, the FBI did not evaluate overall participant feedback regarding this conference and we were also unable to do so.

We also interviewed the Coordinators at the eight FBI field offices regarding the training they received. Two of the eight Coordinators told us they would like the FBI to provide more Coordinator-focused training and direct guidance on official Coordinator duties. The other six Coordinators made no comments about a need for more training on their duties.

In February 2008, TFOS provided a voluntary training opportunity that allowed each Coordinator to be detailed to TFOS's offices at FBI Headquarters. The detail would have provided the Coordinators with a strategic perspective of TFOS as they rotated through most of the TFOS organization. TFOS intended that upon completion of the training rotation each Coordinator would be in a better position to perform their role within their respective field office and law enforcement and intelligence communities.

We interviewed TFOS officials and the field office Coordinators to assess Coordinators' participation in this training. However, TFOS officials we interviewed were unable to provide precise information regarding the training or documentation related to the program. Moreover, none of the Coordinators we interviewed participated in the training rotation. Consequently, we were unable to assess the adequacy of this training.[25]

Given the training needs identified by two of the eight Coordinators we interviewed, and considering the missing conference evaluation documentation, we believe that TFOS should develop and implement a

---

[25] We could not review the program. None of the FBI Headquarter staff we interviewed could provide us with any information on the program, and none of the Coordinators we interviewed participated in the program.

method to evaluate the adequacy of training provided to the field office Coordinators. The Coordinators should receive routine training that focuses on the financial-related investigative techniques and the benefits of the results achieved when these techniques are used. The training the coordinators receive enables them to provide training to the field offices, which strengthens the FBI's ability to enhance the financial aspect of its counterterrorism investigations.

Provision of Coordination and Technical Assistance

Each Coordinator serves as the point-of-contact regarding financial investigative matters that involve interaction between TFOS and FBI field offices. A coordinated approach to terrorist financing investigations is critical because investigations in one office may be linked to investigations in other field offices or countries. As the point-of-contact between the field office and TFOS, the Coordinator should enhance the FBI's ability to coordinate the financial aspects of counterterrorism investigations and criminal matters that could have a potential link to terrorism.

TFOS recommended in a March 2008 electronic communication that each Coordinator assist Special Agents in making contact with TFOS to help field office staff understand the financial services that TFOS can provide. We interviewed Coordinators to determine the extent the Coordinators provided assistance to the field offices. Each Coordinator told us he or she provided assistance to the field office staff. For example, one Coordinator told us that he advised Special Agents when to perform credit checks of investigation subjects and that he analyzed bank documents for Special Agents in cases where the subject was believed to have transmitted funds to finance terrorism. Other Coordinators told us that they periodically received requests for information from TFOS related to counterterrorism cases and performed follow-up on TFOS's requests for information.

TFOS also recommended the Coordinator assist Special Agents in identifying potential terrorist financing matters and then refer the Special Agents to the appropriate components within the field office. Each of the eight Coordinators we interviewed told us they provided some form of technical assistance within their respective field offices such as providing the JTTFs with guidance on the financial aspects of their terrorism investigations. This type of assistance appears consistent with the guidance from TFOS's March 2008 communication.

In a February 2008 communication, TFOS encouraged each Coordinator to train members of the Joint Terrorism Task Force, counterterrorism investigators, and analysts regarding the importance of the financial aspects of terrorism investigations and other information that could be beneficial to their investigations. In addition, TFOS established the Coordinator role as a means to provide financial investigative resources to the field offices. Of the eight Coordinators we interviewed, seven told us they provided or coordinated training within their field offices. One Coordinator told us he did not provide or coordinate terrorist-financing training and did not know if the Special Agents within the field office received this training elsewhere. He also said that this expectation had not been communicated to him, and he did not have time to perform this duty because of his caseload and other work responsibilities.

Review of Counterterrorism and Criminal Cases

In a February 2008 electronic communication, TFOS recommended that each Coordinator review the counterterrorism cases within their respective field offices to identify appropriate financial aspects of cases that merit further financial investigation. Three Coordinators told us they performed this review while five coordinators told us they did not. One Coordinator told us he did not have time to perform reviews of other Special Agents' case files given his own caseload. Another Coordinator said he only reviewed case files from his own squad, and another said that he only reviewed case files for other squads when approached with a request for assistance. Another Coordinator told us that he was not told anything about his duties from TFOS or his field office supervisor.

Additionally, TFOS recommended that each Coordinator identify criminal cases within the field office for a potential link to terrorist financing activity. Of the eight Coordinators we interviewed, three told us they performed this review while the remaining five told us they did not perform this review. One Coordinator told us that he only performed this duty on his own caseload. Another Coordinator told us that because of his own caseload, he did not have time to identify criminal case files assigned to other Special Agents.

The FBI intended for the Coordinator position to play a pivotal role in ensuring that terrorist financing matters were part of the counterterrorism investigations. The FBI established the Coordinator position to enhance the financial aspect of the counterterrorism investigations by identifying potential terrorist financing matters and reviewing cases to identify appropriate financial aspects that merit further financial-related investigative techniques.

For the 209 cases files we reviewed, we assessed documentation maintained in the case files for interaction between the field office

Coordinator and case agents. We reviewed the case files for documentation that supported the Coordinator's review of the sample cases and found evidence that the Coordinators participated in 5 percent of the case files we reviewed. From our case file review, it appears the Coordinators may not be completing this duty as intended by the FBI. Coordinator involvement with the counterterrorism investigations provides the FBI with the ability to ensure field offices include an appropriate financial focus. If the Coordinators are not performing as intended, field offices may not employ appropriate financial-related investigative techniques and achieve the mandatory financial focus.

A TFOS official told us that in practice the Coordinators often do not have time to independently review other Special Agents' counterterrorism case files. The official added that the newly implemented reorganization of TFOS would make it unnecessary for the coordinator to review counterterrorism cases because TFOS staff would perform this review as part of their program manager responsibilities. The reorganization of TFOS is discussed later in this report.

We believe the FBI should better define for its field offices the extent to which Coordinators be assigned to other duties. Reducing the collateral duties assigned to Coordinators should allow the Coordinators to focus on the review of case files for where our audit results indicate improvements could be made.

Liaison with the Financial Community

According to the March 2008 guidance, as liaisons with the local banking community, Coordinators are expected to attend bank fraud working group or criminal task force meetings and to initiate personal contacts within the financial community. We interviewed the Coordinators to determine the extent of their involvement with their respective local financial community. Five of the eight Coordinators told us they interacted with their local financial community while the remaining three told us they did not. We believe the financial community to be vital in the FBI's efforts to address terrorist financing and that the Coordinators should routinely interact with the financial community. By establishing relationships within the financial community, the Coordinators can obtain valuable resources that may lead to the development of cases and provide assistance with ongoing terrorist financing investigations.

FBI-Proposed Changes to the Terrorist Financing Coordinator Initiative

After we completed our audit work and assessment of the Coordinator program, TFOS officials informed us that they had completed a review of the program and prepared a report dated February 2010. That report, produced by a Terrorist Financing Coordinator Working Group (Coordinator Working Group), noted that:

- the Coordinator's job description and duties were not clearly defined;

- Coordinators received inconsistent support from FBI field managers and were spending less than 10 percent of their time working on Coordinator-related matters;

- Coordinators had very little vested interest in the position and there was no mechanism to hold Coordinators accountable for their performance; and

- field offices did not always select the most qualified individual to assume the Coordinator role.

These results are consistent with our findings that coordinators did not always perform their duties as intended by the FBI, performed unrelated collateral duties, and were not always selected in accordance with TFOS guidance.

Based on its review, the Coordinator Working Group recommended that the FBI re-evaluate coordinator duties based on the size of the field office, tie each field office's performance score to terrorist financing so that managers allow Coordinators more time on Coordinator duties, and designate as Coordinators only persons with financial backgrounds.[26] The working group proposed that Coordinators support cases, serve as the TFOS point of contact, and act as liaisons to the financial community. Case support included assessing ongoing and newly opened preliminary and full counterterrorism investigations to ensure appropriate investigative steps are documented. TFOS point of contact duties included providing training to JTTF staff, coordinating trends and initiatives, and explaining the responsibilities of TFOS. As financial community liaison, coordinators would serve as an active member of the Suspicious Activity Review Team,

---

[26] The FBI Inspections Division measures field office performance using a process called a Semi Annual Program Review (SAPR). The Coordinator Working Group recommended that 8 percent of a field office's SAPR score relate to terrorist financing.

participate in local bank security officers meetings, and provide training to local law enforcement and bank security officers on trends in terrorist financing.

The Coordinator Working Group's recommendations were appropriate given the FBI's intent in establishing the Terrorist Financing Coordinator Initiative. The recommended actions would strengthen the Coordinators' engagement with counterterrorism investigations, enhance JTTF staff training on terrorist financing, and help ensure management support to improve program effectiveness. However, TFOS had not implemented the recommendations proposed by the Coordinator Working Group because the FBI planned to restructure TFOS, and as discussed later in this report, make changes to the Coordinator program.

Through a May 2011 memorandum sent to field offices, TFOS officially modified the coordinator's roles and responsibilities. Prior to the restructure, TFOS relied exclusively on Coordinators to assist in providing case review and support functions to counterterrorism investigations now handled by TFOS program managers. TFOS acknowledged that this case review responsibility yielded inconsistent results. As a result, TFOS modified the Coordinator's responsibilities to stress their role as a liaison and conduit of information between TFOS and the field offices, and decrease their case review responsibility.

We believe it is important that all criminal and counterterrorism cases be reviewed for a potential nexus to terrorist financing so that FBI management can seek to achieve a consistent approach to applying financial-related investigative techniques. If the Coordinators are not going to provide such a review of all criminal and counterterrorism cases not reviewed by TFOS, the FBI should ensure another mechanism to achieve these reviews.

TFOS Involvement

During our review of 209 counterterrorism cases, we sought documentation of TFOS's coordination and involvement in these investigations. Specifically, we reviewed cases for TFOS coordination and involvement with financial-related products, such as record analyses, linkage charts, data base checks, or electronic communications provided in response to requests made by the field offices. We also reviewed case files to determine if TFOS made any recommendations regarding financial-related investigative techniques. Of the 209 cases we reviewed, 24 contained documentation of coordination with TFOS. Of these, 14 cases showed TFOS provided a financial product such as record analyses, linkage charts, and database checks and 10 cases contained documentation of TFOS providing recommendations.

Of the 40 Special Agents we interviewed, 19 told us they had not worked with TFOS during their counterterrorism investigations. The 19 field Special Agents provided various explanations for why they had not interacted with TFOS. For example, one Special Agent told us that his office was self-sufficient. Another told us that he worked on a reactive squad, and his cases did not reach the point of needing TFOS.

For the 21 Special Agents we interviewed who had worked with TFOS, 15 had positive experiences and believed TFOS was helpful and provided beneficial and timely assistance. For example, one Special Agent said that when he asked TFOS staff for special record searches they were helpful and timely. Another said that TFOS was responsive when asked for assistance. When requesting TFOS's assistance for a 2006 case, a Special Agent told us that TFOS staff conducted interviews, wrote an affidavit in support of forfeiture, and conducted records checks, which he considered beneficial. Another described one of her cases in which a TFOS analyst was assigned full-time and was very responsive.

The reasons agents provided for not having positive interactions with TFOS included a perception that TFOS was only interested in high profile cases and a perception that TFOS was unresponsive and when it did respond, its assistance was not useful.

We believe a negative experience with TFOS or the lack of assistance from TFOS when requested can distract the field Special Agents from focusing on the financial aspects of the counterterrorism investigations. The FBI should clarify when TFOS assistance should be expected or when the assistance should come from another person such as a financial analyst or the Coordinator.

Lack of Communication on Case Management

TFOS officials told us they understand that some field Special Agents may not have received the assistance requested in the past because TFOS experienced several management changes in recent years and each new Section Chief brought in a new focus on the section's approach to addressing terrorist financing.

In August 2010, the Assistant Director of the Counterterrorism Division told us that he planned to assign TFOS staff members program manager status over certain counterterrorism investigation cases. Prior to these changes, TFOS acted in a supportive rather than a directive role at the headquarters level and TFOS staff members could not manage the techniques Special Agents employed in their counterterrorism investigations. However, the Counterterrorism Division's International Terrorism Operation Section (ITOS) could mandate such changes. ITOS program managers are organized into teams led by a Supervisory Special Agent. ITOS teams approve actions in counterterrorism investigations and monitor the progression of the cases. TFOS officials told us the lack of ownership by TFOS over counterterrorism investigations limited the assistance TFOS staff could provide to field Special Agents on daily financial matters, such as analyzing bank records. As discussed below, this change was initiated in December 2010 when TFOS was restructured.

TFOS Restructure

The primary goal of restructuring TFOS was to transform the section and integrate strategic intelligence, develop processes to enhance counterterrorism investigations, and initiate operational program management. Since December 2010, TFOS staff members have program manager status over fundraiser counterterrorism investigations whereas previously they were unable to ensure that financial-related investigative techniques were incorporated into these investigations. As program managers, TFOS staff is able to approve actions and direct field Special Agents to use certain tactics, such as financial-related investigative techniques, in an investigation. This change should reduce the limitation TFOS officials told us they had in managing counterterrorism investigations. According to the FBI, TFOS has gone through a major transformation into a fully operational section, actively involved in the program management of the FBI's terrorist financing investigations. TFOS' program management efforts include daily contact with field office and liaison partners to fully support investigative demands and threat mitigation. However, the requirement remains that every pending and full counterterrorism investigation has a financial focus. We believe the FBI should ensure that counterterrorism investigations not managed by TFOS continue to undergo close review for financial leads.

In May 2011, TFOS established official duties and responsibilities for the Coordinator program that decreased Coordinators' involvement in case reviews. Coordinator duties and responsibilities should be re-evaluated to ensure field offices do not under-utilize the resources provided to enhance the financial aspects of counterterrorism investigations. Specifically, Coordinators should continue to perform case reviews and identify criminal cases with a financial nexus. This provides field Special Agents with direct resources and enhances counterterrorism investigations.

Conclusion

We found that Special Agents utilized financial-related investigative techniques while conducting counterterrorism investigations. However, the FBI can improve its terrorist financing program by requiring Special Agents to better document their use and valid reasons for not using the six financial-related investigative techniques recommended by the FBI's Terrorist Financing Operations Section. We found that documentation was not always readily identifiable in the case files to support the use of or valid reasons for not using the techniques. Better documentation for the use of the techniques would enhance the FBI's ability to assess whether Special Agents focused on the financial aspects of all counterterrorism investigations and ensure more-effective continuation of investigations when a case is transferred or reassigned. Over half of the Special Agents interviewed did not believe the use of the sub-file encouraged their use of the financial-related investigative techniques. We believe the sub-file encourages focus and organization to the financial aspect of counterterrorism investigations and assists in ensuring that Special Agents give appropriate attention to the financial aspects of each preliminary and full counterterrorism investigation. We believe Special Agents' interest in these techniques could be improved through routine financial investigative training and increased TFOS involvement.

Further, field offices did not use the Terrorist Financing Coordinators as the FBI intended. Particularly, we found during the review period that Terrorist Financing Coordinators did not routinely review counterterrorism cases to ensure the field offices implemented the financial focus directive for counterterrorism investigations.

To enhance the FBI's efforts to identify, investigate, and connect terrorist financing activities, the FBI should ensure that Special Agents include documented support in the case file for the use and valid reasons for not using the financial-related investigative techniques, that field offices support the use of the financial sub-file, and that its Terrorist Financing Coordinators are more engaged in their field office's counterterrorism investigations.

Recommendations

We recommend that the FBI:

1. Ensure Special Agents appropriately document their use of all financial-related investigative techniques for all counterterrorism investigations.

2. Consider requiring Special Agents to document the valid reasons for not using the six basic financial-related investigative techniques for all counterterrorism investigations.

3. Ensure Special Agents adhere to the requirement for the creation of the mandatory financial investigative sub-file for all counterterrorism investigations.

4. Ensure that Special Agents in the field offices with responsibility for counterterrorism investigations receive on-going training regarding financial-related investigative techniques.

5. Clearly define the roles, responsibilities, and expectations of the Terrorist Financing Coordinators.

6. Develop, implement, and document formal methods to evaluate the Terrorist Financing Coordinator Conference and other training provided to Coordinators.

7. Ensure that there are appropriate written qualifications and training for the field offices' selection of a Terrorist Financing Coordinator as defined by TFOS.

8. Ensure that management develops a consistent approach for field offices to include financial-related focus and organization for all counterterrorism investigations.

II. THE FBI'S AND NSD'S COORDINATION AND SHARING EFFORTS REGARDING TERRORIST FINANCING OPERATIONS

The Department's counterterrorism strategy involves the use and sharing of intelligence by working with federal, state, and local partners, as well as international entities. The Department's approach to counterterrorism involves a focus on all components of terrorist organizations, including terrorist financing. We found that the FBI and NSD utilize established mechanisms and relationships for counterterrorism matters to share and coordinate terrorist financing-related information and operations.

The Department's Counterterrorism Approach

The Department's overall approach to counterterrorism involves the investigation of the entire terrorist organization, with terrorist financing as a subset of the investigation. Terrorist financing matters are considered during investigations and intelligence gathering, along with a wide array of other terrorist activities. During our audit, we identified mechanisms used by the FBI and NSD to coordinate and share counterterrorism intelligence that encompass terrorist financing and other aspects of terrorist operations.

FBI Coordination and Sharing Efforts

As part of its central mission, the FBI provides leadership and criminal justice services to federal, state, and local agencies. According to *The Attorney General's Guidelines for Domestic FBI Operations*, the FBI may disseminate information obtained or produced through activities under these guidelines to other federal, state, local, or tribal agencies if relevant to its responsibilities. One of the FBI's top priorities is to support these law enforcement agencies in performing counterterrorism investigations. These agencies receive information and resources that include terrorist financing intelligence from the FBI's 56 field offices and 400 smaller resident agency offices throughout the United States.

The FBI also participates with domestic and international entities to coordinate activities related to terrorist financing. Various FBI offices and programs, such as the Joint Terrorism Task Forces, Terrorist Financing Operations Section, and Legal Attaché Offices share in the effort to target terrorist financing.[27]

---

[27] Legal Attaché Offices, also known as Legats, are FBI offices located in U.S. embassies around the world.

Since the 2001 terrorist attacks, the FBI has sought to implement an intelligence program to analyze and share a broad range of counterterrorism information. To assess the FBI's coordination and sharing activities pertaining to terrorist financing, we focused our audit work on the efforts of TFOS, the Joint Terrorism Task Force, and the FBI's interactions with the Department of Homeland Security. While we recognize that overall FBI coordination and sharing efforts are more broadly based, we selected these areas of focus because they form the core of the FBI's terrorist financing investigative efforts. The FBI Office of the General Counsel provided us with information regarding the FBI's authority for combating terrorist financing. The Terrorist Financing Operations Section, Joint Terrorism Task Forces, FBI field offices, Legal Attachés, and the Department of Homeland Security were included as entities to address terrorist financing.

TFOS Coordination with Other Agencies

One of the key objectives of TFOS is to coordinate joint participation, liaison, and outreach efforts so that the FBI appropriately utilizes the financial information resources of private, government, and foreign entities. To accomplish this objective, TFOS engages in various programs and initiatives with the private sector, intelligence community, and international community. We reviewed these programs and initiatives to assess the extent to which TFOS engages in appropriate coordination.

One of the FBI's goals in establishing TFOS was to form an international law enforcement body to address terrorist financing. Thus, TFOS engages in extensive coordination with authorities of numerous foreign governments in terrorist financing matters that leads to joint investigative efforts throughout the world. Through international and government liaison efforts, TFOS established partnerships with foreign law enforcement. For example, the FBI established a Joint Task Force on Terrorism Financing with Saudi Arabia. A TFOS staff member also has been assigned to London's New Scotland Yard Metropolitan Police Department's National Terrorist Financing Investigation Unit.

The FBI also participates in the Terrorist Financing Working Group, led by the Department of State, which coordinates government efforts to identify, prioritize, assess, and assist countries whose financial systems are vulnerable to terrorist exploitation.[28] Regarding training, TFOS staff members are often presenters at state-funded training conferences. TFOS also developed a specific financing and money laundering crimes curriculum

---

[28] The Terrorist Financing Working Group includes members from the Departments of State, the Treasury, Justice, and Homeland Security.

for international training, which includes topics such as: (1) acquiring and handling evidence in a document-intensive financial investigation, (2) major case management techniques, (3) forensic examination tools, and (4) methods of terrorist financing. TFOS officials also represent the United States in meetings with the Financial Action Task Force.[29]

TFOS International Training

The FBI's Legal Attaché offices or "Legats" assist it in addressing the global nature of terrorist financing. As of April 2011, there were 63 FBI Legal Attaché offices working with foreign law enforcement and security agencies to coordinate investigations of interest to both the host country and the United States.[30] The FBI uses the Legal Attaché offices' expertise to make use of the financial information from international law enforcement. TFOS staff members, along with the Legal Attaché offices, conduct training to foreign countries on financial-related investigative techniques.

International training is a key program of the FBI's international operations to enhance information sharing. International training teaches foreign law enforcement officers how to perform basic and advanced investigative techniques and principles that promote cooperation and aid in the collection of evidence. According to the Section Chief of the Office of International Operations, Legal Attachés first identify the need for training regarding terrorist financing matters in their host countries. TFOS conducted 15 of these international training sessions in 13 countries in 2009 and 21 international training sessions in 17 countries in 2010.

Counterterrorism Squad on Joint Terrorism Task Force

Through the Joint Terrorism Task Forces (JTTF), local, state, and federal law enforcement agencies work together to address terrorism on a regional scale. Over 600 state and local agencies and 50 federal agencies participate in the JTTFs, which have more than 4,000 members nationwide. The FBI leads each JTTF in investigating terrorist activities that include terrorist financing activities. FBI agents, analysts, and other professional support staff join with task force officers to form counterterrorism squads.

---

[29] The Financial Action Task Force (FATF) is an inter-governmental body whose purpose is the development and promotion of national and international policies to combat money laundering and terrorist financing. The FATF is a policymaking body that works to generate the necessary political will to bring about legislative and regulatory reforms in these areas. The FATF has published 49 recommendations to meet this objective.

[30] Appendix III provides a global map of the locations for the Legat offices.

Non-FBI JTTF members are assigned to and serve as co-lead agents on counterterrorism squads. They function similarly to assigned FBI Special Agents in that they attend squad meetings and have their own caseloads. We interviewed 35 personnel from non-FBI JTTF member agencies during our fieldwork at 8 FBI field offices, as illustrated in Exhibit 9. When asked about TFOS involvement in their work, one non-FBI JTTF member told us he had received training from TFOS. Two members said that they had reached out to TFOS for help on a case. In one of these cases, the member sent case information to TFOS, but 6 months later was informed TFOS could not help. The other member said he was still waiting for TFOS assistance.

Exhibit 7: List of Law Enforcement Agencies Interviewed

FBI Field Office	Law Enforcement Agency
Atlanta Field Office	Atlanta Police Department
Chicago Field Office	Chicago Police Department Alcohol, Tobacco, Firearms, and Explosives Homeland Security Investigations Internal Revenue Service U.S. Coast Guard U.S. Customs and Border Protection U.S. Secret Service
Detroit Field Office	Dearborn Police Department Detroit Police Department Immigration and Customs Enforcement Internal Revenue Service U.S. Customs and Border Protection
Houston Field Office	Houston Police Department Immigration and Customs Enforcement Internal Revenue Service U.S. Customs and Border Protection
Los Angeles Field Office	Alcohol, Tobacco, Firearms and Explosives Drug Enforcement Administration Immigration and Customs Enforcement Internal Revenue Service Los Angeles Police Department

Miami Field Office	City of Boca Raton Police Department
	City of Miami Police Department
	Florida Department of Environment Protection
	Internal Revenue Service
	Miami-Dade Police Department
	Miramar Miami Police Department
New York Field Office	Immigration and Customs Enforcement
	Internal Revenue Service
	New York Police Department
	U.S. Secret Service

Source: OIG JTTF Member Interviews

Immigration and Customs Enforcement

In May 2003, the Attorney General and the Department of Homeland Security (DHS) signed a Memorandum of Agreement (MOA) to resolve conflict, clarify the terrorist financing activities and investigations between the FBI and DHS, and increase information sharing and coordination. According to FBI congressional testimony, the MOA addressed the importance of waging a seamless, coordinated campaign against sources of terrorist financing. In response to the September 11 terrorist attacks, the U.S. Customs Service conducted money laundering and financial crimes investigations.[31] The FBI and U.S. Immigration and Customs Enforcement (ICE) were to detail appropriate personnel to each other's agency and develop specific collaborative procedures to determine whether applicable ICE investigations or financial crime leads may be related to terrorism or terrorist financing. The MOA and its related procedures specified that the FBI was to have the lead role in investigating terrorist financing. ICE was to pursue terrorist financing solely through participation in FBI-led task forces, except as expressly approved by the FBI. Under the MOA, any investigation with a nexus to terrorism that originates at the DHS is transferred to the FBI.

To determine whether ICE financial cases may be related to terrorism or terrorist financing, TFOS and ICE established a Joint Vetting Unit to

---

[31] In 2001, the Department of the Treasury established Operation Green Quest to expand existing counterterrorist efforts by targeting current terrorist funding sources and identifying possible future sources. It also targeted fraudulent charities and the shipment of bulk cash. The U.S. Customs Service was once under the Department of the Treasury. In March 2003, the U.S. Customs Service transferred to the Department of Homeland Security.

minimize conflict and coordinate investigations and projects.[32] According to the MOA, a supervisory ICE agent is detailed to TFOS as a Deputy Section Chief and an FBI Supervisory Special Agent is detailed to ICE in its financial crimes division. This cross management is intended to ensure that each agency has access to all information and that agents are fully integrated in the daily efforts to address terrorist financing.

We interviewed the Deputy Section Chief ICE agent detailed to TFOS. The agent told us that the Joint Vetting Unit is working well at the national level and there had not been any complaints from the JTTF staff regarding case conflicts or sharing. The Deputy Section Chief also told us that ICE has increased FBI access to its databases. In addition to the ICE and Customs and Border Protection databases, ICE began providing information from the Transportation Security Administration databases to the FBI. The FBI continues to share its databases with ICE agents located in the JTTFs.

Based on the details included in the preceding paragraphs, we believe that the FBI and ICE have established a reasonable and beneficial information-sharing arrangement, sharing information at the headquarters level and within the JTTFs.

NSD Coordination and Sharing Efforts

The Department's National Security Division is responsible for ensuring the coordination of all national security matters among the Department's components, including the U.S. Attorneys' Offices and the FBI. NSD intelligence analysts are briefed daily on FBI intelligence. While the NSD does not operate programs or activities specific to terrorist financing, it includes terrorist financing within the scope of its counterterrorism activities. The following section describes the NSD's national coordination efforts.

Anti-Terrorism Advisory Council

In September 2001, the Department directed each U.S. Attorney's Office to form an Anti-Terrorism Advisory Council (ATAC) and directed prosecutors to invite federal and local law enforcement agencies to join the ATAC. The ATAC coordinates specific anti-terrorism initiatives, provide training, and facilitate information sharing with state and local authorities in each federal district in the United States.

---

[32] The Joint Vetting Unit is comprised of ICE and FBI staff that has joint access to FBI and ICE databases. This staff conducts reviews of persons under investigation or other leads to determine whether a potential nexus to terrorism exists.

The NSD's Counterterrorism Section leads the ATAC program and works with the coordinators in each district to form a nationwide information-sharing network. The ATAC program provides training to state and local law enforcement officials. Other FBI Counterterrorism officials also speak during the annual ATAC conferences.

We interviewed the National ATAC coordinator and seven ATAC coordinators representing the Eastern District of Michigan; the Southern Districts of Florida, Texas, New York, and California; and the Northern Districts of Illinois and Georgia. The ATAC coordinators interact regularly with the NSD on the status of counterterrorism investigations and investigative strategies for particular cases. Three of the seven ATAC coordinators we interviewed had worked on terrorist financing cases. The ATAC coordinators told us that the NSD is helpful and they are satisfied with the NSD's assistance.

Designation of Terrorist Groups

On behalf of the Attorney General, the NSD assists the Departments of State and the Treasury in designating individuals, groups, or entities as terrorists to freeze their assets or property in order to prevent the commission of future terrorist acts.[33] Ultimately, the terrorist designation denies individuals or organizations access to the U.S. financial system and it notifies the public and the world that these parties are engaged in supporting terrorism or are associated with terrorists and their organizations. Designation is intended to counter terrorism by exposing terrorist financing money trails that may generate leads to previously unknown terrorist cells and financiers. In addition, designation can potentially dismantle terrorist financing networks by encouraging designated persons to disassociate themselves from terrorist activity and renounce their affiliation with terrorist groups and their support networks. The Secretary of State is primarily responsible for the designation of Foreign Terrorist Organizations (FTO), under the authority of section 219 of the *Immigration and Nationality Act*.

FTO designations are made after an extensive interagency review process in which information about an entity's activity, taken both from classified and open sources, are scrutinized. The NSD, which represents the

---

[33] The designation process involves having a reasonable basis or reasonable grounds to suspect or believe that an individual or organization is a terrorist, one who finances terrorism, or a terrorist organization. Upon identification, a freeze is placed on the individual's or organization's assets or property to prevent the commission of future terrorist acts.

Department, along with the Departments of State and Treasury, work with the federal intelligence community to closely review a detailed administrative record that documents the terrorist activity of the proposed designee to ensure that the record supports adequately the factual findings required by the applicable authority and to assess litigation risk in the event a designation subsequently is challenged by the designated entity. The designation of an entity as an FTO is made based on information contained in the administrative record. The administrative record is a compilation of classified and unclassified information that demonstrates whether the statutory criteria for designation have been satisfied. The Department of State notifies Congress 7 days before publishing an FTO designation in the Federal Register. As of January 2012, there were 49 FTO designations.

An official from the Department of State, Office of Law Enforcement and Intelligence, Office of the Legal Advisor, described the working relationship between the Department of State and the NSD as good. This attorney told us the NSD reviews the administrative record of proposed designees in a timely manner. In instances of non-concurrence during the first review, the NSD and the Departments of State and Treasury work together to revise the administrative record to ensure that the case for designation is legally sufficient and can withstand judicial challenge.

The Departments of State and Treasury share the responsibility for designations of Specially Designated Global Terrorists (SDGT), including those done under Executive Order 13224 issued pursuant to the *International Emergency Economic Powers Act*. Designation as an SDGT permits the prosecution of a person who willfully engages in unlicensed financial transactions with designated persons and organizations and authorizes the Department of the Treasury to block assets and freeze bank accounts of those designated groups and individuals.

As of December 31, 2010, the SDGT list of 578 individuals and entities includes all of the organizations on the State Department's FTO list. Unlike the FTO list, the SDGT list of designated entities is not limited to foreign groups.

Based on our review, it appears that the NSD has appropriate processes in place to coordinate efforts regarding terrorist financing. The NSD's Counterterrorism Section is sharing information on different levels within the Department and is communicating with agencies outside of the Department.

FBI and NSD Joint Coordination and Sharing Efforts

The Attorney General's Guidelines for Domestic FBI Operations require the FBI to consult regularly with the NSD to exchange advice and information concerning threats to national security. The guidelines also require the FBI to: (1) notify the NSD of full investigations that involve foreign intelligence collection or investigations of U.S. persons in relation to threats to national security; (2) provide the NSD information about its foreign intelligence collection program, including information regarding the scope and nature of foreign intelligence collection activities in each FBI field office; and (3) provide the NSD access to information obtained in national security or foreign intelligence activities. The Assistant Attorney General for National Security also has the general authority to obtain reports from the FBI concerning these activities.

We interviewed NSD officials to determine the extent to which they coordinate and share information with the FBI. We found that intelligence and investigative information is shared at multiple management levels within the NSD and elsewhere within the Department. The Attorney General, the Deputy Attorney General, the FBI Director, and the Assistant Attorney General for National Security meet every morning to receive a threat briefing and to discuss ongoing investigations. NSD attorneys and FBI supervisors meet weekly with FBI counterparts to discuss pending matters and investigative strategies in particular cases. NSD officials hold regular meetings with the FBI to discuss terrorism-related matters where they advise the FBI on their terrorist investigations in matters such as determining which legal tools to use to collect and preserve evidence. Additionally, NSD officials participate in two daily intelligence meetings with other federal agencies that make up the federal intelligence community, including the FBI.

Coordination with State and Local Agencies

The NSD provides training, general intelligence information, and legal guidance to state and local agencies through its Anti-Terrorism Advisory Council program, as described earlier in this report.

Terrorism Prosecutions

In coordination with the FBI and the U.S. Attorneys' Offices, the NSD assists in the investigation and prosecution of terrorist financing cases by serving as the principal legal advisor concerning questions of law, regulations, and guidelines as well as the legality of domestic and overseas intelligence operations.

Criminal prosecution is a part of the NSD's counterterrorism program. Through its expanded use of criminal statutes available in the federal criminal code, the NSD seeks to use criminal charges available in the federal criminal code to obtain criminal convictions, thereby intervening at the early stages of terrorist planning before a terrorist act occurs. The NSD also authorizes the use of a variety of other methods to prevent terrorist acts from occurring, such as making an arrest or bringing immigration charges.

The material support statutes, 18 U.S.C. §§ 2339A and 2339B, which criminalize the act of knowingly providing support and engaging in financial transactions with terrorists, are a means of disrupting United States-based terrorist supporters and are central to the NSD's efforts to prosecute terrorist financing cases. The NSD draws upon other criminal statutes available in the federal criminal code based upon the facts and circumstance of each case.[34]

From September 11, 2001, to March 18, 2010, the NSD reports that it has been involved in 104 unsealed terrorism-related convictions based on federal criminal statutes prohibiting certain financial transactions, money laundering, and providing material support to terrorists and terrorist organizations, as listed in Appendix V.[35]

Conclusion

FBI and NSD efforts against terrorist financing involve working with federal, state, local, and international entities through programs and initiatives that provide operational support and legal guidance. These coordination and sharing efforts increase terrorist financing training, supports communication between agencies, and designate organizations who seek to commit or support terrorist acts. Our audit work indicates the existence of appropriate coordination and sharing efforts to strengthen partnerships with agencies. Such partnerships may further the Department's achievement of its first goal, to prevent terrorist operations before they occur.

---

[34] Appendix V lists these criminal statutes.

[35] Unsealed records are court decisions that are available for public review.

STATEMENT ON INTERNAL CONTROLS

As required by the *Government Auditing Standards*, we tested, as appropriate, internal controls significant within the context of our audit objectives. A deficiency in an internal control exists when the design or operation of a control does not allow management or employees, in the normal course of performing their assigned functions, to timely prevent or detect: (1) impairments to the effectiveness and efficiency of operations, (2) misstatements in financial or performance information, or (3) violations of laws and regulations. Our evaluation of FBI and NSD internal controls were not made for the purpose of providing assurance on its internal control structure as a whole. FBI and NSD management are responsible for the establishment and maintenance of internal controls.

Through our audit testing, we did not identify deficiencies in the FBI's and NSD's internal controls that were significant within the context of the audit objectives and that, based upon the audit work performed, we believe would affect the FBI's and NSD's ability to effectively and efficiently operate, to correctly state financial and performance information, and to ensure compliance with laws and regulations.

Because we are not expressing an opinion on the FBI's or NSD's internal control structure as a whole, this statement is intended solely for the information and use of the FBI and NSD. This restriction is not intended to limit the distribution of this report, which is a matter of public record.

STATEMENT ON COMPLIANCE WITH
LAWS AND REGULATIONS

As required by the *Government Auditing Standards* we tested, as appropriate given our audit scope and objectives, selected transactions, records, procedures, and practices, to obtain reasonable assurance that the FBI and NSD management complied with federal laws and regulations, for which noncompliance, in our judgment, could have a material effect on the results of our audit. The FBI's and NSD's management are responsible for ensuring compliance with applicable federal laws and regulations. In planning our audit, we identified the following laws and regulations that concerned the operations of the FBI and NSD that were significant within the context of the audit objectives:

- USA PATRIOT Improvement and Reauthorization Act of 2005
- International Emergency Economic Powers Act
- Section 219 of the Immigration and Nationality Act

Our audit included examining, on a test basis, the FBI's and NSD's compliance with the aforementioned laws and regulations that could have a material effect on the FBI's and NSD's operations, through interviewing personnel, analyzing data, assessing internal control procedures, and examining procedural practices. Nothing came to our attention that the FBI and NSD did not comply with the aforementioned laws and regulations.

Audit Objectives, Scope, and Methodology

Objectives

The objectives of this audit were to determine if the FBI and NSD: (1) have implemented appropriate programs to identify, investigate, and prosecute terrorist financing activities; and (2) appropriately coordinated and shared information regarding terrorist financing operations.

Scope and Methodology

We conducted this performance audit in accordance with Generally Accepted Government Auditing Standards. Those standards require that we plan and perform the audit to obtain sufficient, appropriate evidence to provide a reasonable basis for our findings and conclusions based on our audit objectives. We believe that the evidence obtained provides a reasonable basis for our findings and conclusions based on our audit objectives. We performed fieldwork at FBI and NSD Headquarters located in Washington, D.C., and the following FBI field offices:

Atlanta Field Office	Atlanta, Georgia
Chicago Field Office	Chicago, Illinois
Detroit Field Office	Detroit, Michigan
Houston Field Office	Houston, Texas
Los Angeles Field Office	Los Angeles, California
Miami Field Office	Miami, Florida
New York Field Office	New York, New York
Washington Field Office	Washington, D.C.

We selected field offices based on the amount of time Special Agents recorded performing counterterrorism activities for FY 2010. From the 10 offices with the highest level of recorded counterterrorism activity, we selected 7 offices from diverse locations throughout the United States. In addition, we also selected the Atlanta Field Office because of its close proximity to the OIG Atlanta Regional Audit Office that conducted this audit.

The audit focused on the FBI's National Security Branch, Counterterrorism Division, and Terrorist Financing Operations Section (TFOS) and the National Security Division's Counterterrorism Sections.

To accomplish the audit objectives, we interviewed FBI and NSD Headquarters officials regarding their approach to address terrorist financing and their efforts to coordinate and share information on terrorist financing operations.

To determine the extent to which Special Agents used TFOS's recommended financial-related investigative techniques and opened the mandatory sub-files, we reviewed case files at FBI field offices in Atlanta, Chicago, Detroit, Houston, Los Angeles, Miami, New York, and Washington, D.C. We began our testing in the Atlanta and Washington, D.C. field offices where we initially selected a judgmental sample of 35 and a random sample of 15 counterterrorism cases during FY 2006 through FY 2010.

Based on that initial work, we refined our sampling and testing technique. For each of the remaining six FBI field offices, we obtained a universe of opened and closed counterterrorism cases for FY 2008 through FY 2010. For each of the 6 offices, we elected to test 9 cases from each of the 3 fiscal years, for a total of 27 cases for each office. As a result, we elected to test 162 additional counterterrorism cases for the 6 offices. We selected random numbers for our case sample and then used these random numbers to select 27 case files from each of the 6 universes of counterterrorism cases provided by the FBI. We required that each sample for the six field offices include a minimum of five terrorist financing cases. The FBI confirmed the designated terrorist financing cases include in our sample.

Our total sample for the 8 FBI field offices was 212. Of the 212 counterterrorism cases included in our sample, we could not test 3 cases for the following reasons.

- In the Los Angeles Field Office, the coordinator told us that the field office assigned an investigation case number based on information obtained from a legal attaché, but the office did not investigate the case and subsequently closed it without any action completed.[36]

- In the Miami Field Office, an FBI official told us the office inadvertently opened a counterterrorism case and performed no activity on it. We observed that the case file folder was stapled shut and no documents were inside the case file.

---

[36] The FBI has offices worldwide called Legal Attachés or Legats located in U.S. embassies. Appendix III shows a map of the Legat offices.

- In the New York Field Office, the office staff merged one case with another. There were no documents to review for one of the merged cases.

We conducted a two-stage review of the 209 sampled case files. During fieldwork, we performed an initial review of the sampled case files for documentary support. The FBI subsequently provided additional documentation and we performed a second review of the sampled case files. Our sampling design and methodology was not designed to project our audit test results to the universe counterterrorism cases.

The NSD is responsible for coordinating the Department's national security efforts among the components of the Department, the intelligence community and other federal agencies; state, local, and foreign governments; and outside organizations. We interviewed officials within the Department, the Department of State, and U.S. Attorneys' Offices to discuss their relationships with the NSD.

Abbreviations

Abbreviation	Description
ATAC	Anti-Terrorism Advisory Council
CTD	Counterterrorism Division
CPI	Crime Problem Indicator
DHS	Department of Homeland Security
FATF	Financial Action Task Force
FBI	Federal Bureau of Investigation
FinCEN	Financial Crimes Enforcement Network
FTO	Foreign Terrorist Organization
GAO	Government Accountability Office
HLF	Holy Land Foundation for Relief and Development
ICE	U.S. Immigration and Customs Enforcement
IEEPA	International Emergency Economic Powers Act
ITOS	International Terrorism Operations Section
JTTF	Joint Terrorism Task Force
MOA	Memorandum of Agreement
NSD	National Security Division
OIG	Office of the Inspector General
SAR	Suspicious Activity Report
SDGT	Specially Designated Global Terrorist
TFOS	Terrorist Financing Operations Section
TFRG	Terrorism Financing Review Group

FBI Legal Attaché Offices

Africa
Algiers, Algeria
Addis Ababa, Ethiopia
Cairo, Egypt
Dakar, Senegal
Freetown, Sierra Leone
Lagos, Nigeria
Nairobi, Kenya
Pretoria, South Africa
Rabat, Morocco

Americas
Bogota, Columbia
Brasilia, Brazil
Bridgetown, Barbados
Buenos Aires, Argentina
Caracas, Venezuela
Mexico City, Mexico
Ottawa, Canada
Panama City, Panama
Santiago, Chile
Santo Domingo, Dom. Republic
San Salvador, El Salvador

Asia
Bangkok, Thailand
Beijing, China
Canberra, Australia
Hong Kong, China
Jakarta, Indonesia
Kuala Lumpur, Malaysia
Manila, Philippines
New Delhi, India
Phnon Penh, Cambodia
Seoul, South Korea
Singapore, Singapore
Tokyo, Japan

Eurasia
Astana, Kazakhstan
Ankara, Turkey
Athens, Greece
Bucharest, Romania
Budapest, Hungary
Kyiv, Ukraine
Moscow, Russia
Sarajevo, Bosnia-Herzegovina
Sofia, Bulgaria
Tallinn, Estonia
Tbilisi, Georgia
Warsaw, Poland

Europe
Berlin, Germany
Bern, Switzerland
Brussels, Belgium
Copenhagen,
  Denmark
London, England
Madrid, Spain
Paris, France
Rome, Italy
The Hague,
  Netherlands
Vienna, Austria

Middle East
Abu Dhabi, UAE
Amman, Jordan
Baghdad, Iraq
Doha, Qatar
Islamabad, Pakistan
Kabul, Afghanistan
Riyadh, Saudi Arabia
Sanaa, Yemen
Tel Aviv, Israel

Source: FBI website

Designated Foreign Terrorist Organizations

1. Abu Nidal Organization (ANO)
2. Abu Sayyaf Group (ASG)
3. Al-Aqsa Martyrs Brigade (AAMS)
4. Al-Shabaab
5. Ansar al-Islam (AAI)
6. Asbat al-Ansar
7. Aum Shinrikyo (AUM)
8. Basque Fatherland and Liberty (ETA)
9. Communist Party of the Philippines/New People's Army (CPP/NPA)
10. Continuity Irish Republican Army (CIRA)
11. Gama'a al-Islamiyya (Islamic Group)
12. HAMAS (Islamic Resistance Movement)
13. Harakat ul-Jihad-i-Islami/Banglasdesh (HUJI-B)
14. Harakat ul-Mujahidin (HUM)
15. Hizballah (Party of God)
16. Islamic Jihad Union (IJU)
17. Islamic Movement of Uzbekistan (IMU)
18. Jaish-e-Mohammed (JEM) (Army of Mohammed)
19. Jemaah Islamiya organization (JI)
20. Kahane Chai (Kach)
21. Kata'ib Hizballah (KH)
22. Kongra-Gel (KGK, formerly Kurdistan Worker's Party, PKK, KADEK)
23. Lashkar-e Tayyiba (LT) (Army of Righteous)
24. Lashkar i Jhangvi (LJ)
25. Liberation Tigers of Tamil Eelam (LTTE)
26. Libyan Islamic Fighting Group (LIFG)
27. Moroccan Islamic Combatant Group (GICM)
28. Mujahedin-e Khalq Organization (MEK)
29. National Liberation Army (ELN)
30. Palestine Liberation Front (PLF)
31. Palestinian Islamic Jihad (PIJ)
32. Popular Front for the Liberation of Palestine (PFLP)
33. PFLP – General Command (PFLP – GC)
34. al-Qaida in Iraq (AQI)
35. al-Qa'ida
36. al- Qa'ida in the Arabian Peninsula (AQAP)
37. al-Qaida in the Islamic Maghreb (formerly GSPC)
38. Real IRA (RIRA)
39. Revolutionary Armed Forces of Colombia (FARC)
40. Revolutionary Organization 17 November (17N)
41. Revolutionary People's Liberation Party/Front (DHKP/C)
42. Revolutionary Struggle (RS)
43. Shining Path (Sendero Luminoso, SL)
44. United Self-Defense Forces of Colombia (AUC)
45. Harakat-ul Jihad Islami (HUJI)
46. Tehrik-e Taliban Pakistan (TTP)
47. Jundallah
48. Army of Islam (AOI)

Source: Department of State website

Terrorist Statutes Applicable to Financial Transactions, Money Laundering, Material Support to Terrorists, and Terrorist Organizations

United States Code	Description
18 U.S.C. § 226	Bribery affecting port security
18 U.S.C. § 832(a)	Participation in the development of nuclear and other weapons of mass destruction by terrorists
18 U.S.C. § 981	Assets of terrorists organizations
18 U.S.C. § 1956	Laundering of monetary instruments
18 U.S.C. § 1957	Engaging in monetary transactions in property derived from specified unlawful activity
18 U.S.C. § 1960	Unlicensed money transmitting businesses
18 U.S.C. § 2284	Transportation of terrorists
18 U.S.C. § 2332d	Financial transactions with terrorists
18 U.S.C. § 2339	Harboring terrorists
18 U.S.C. § 2339A	Providing material support to terrorists
18 U.S.C. § 2339B	Providing material support to designated terrorist organizations
18 U.S.C. § 2339C	Terrorist financing
18 U.S.C. § 2339D	Receiving military training from a financial terrorist organization
31 U.S.C. § 5322(a)	Currency smuggling
21 U.S.C. § 960a	Narcoterrorism
28 U.S.C. § 2641(c)	Criminal forfeiture
50 U.S.C. § 1701	Unusual and extraordinary threat; declaration of national emergency; exercise of Presidential authorities
50 U.S.C. § 1702	Presidential authorities
50 U.S.C. § 1705(b)	International Emergency Economic Power Act violations/ transactions with designated groups

Source: NSD

THE FEDERAL BUREAU OF INVESTIGATION'S RESPONSE TO THE DRAFT AUDIT REPORT

U.S. Department of Justice

Federal Bureau of Investigation

Washington, D. C. 20535-0001

March 18, 2013

The Honorable Michael E. Horowitz
Inspector General
Office of the Inspector General
U. S. Department of Justice
950 Pennsylvania Avenue, N.W.
Washington, DC 20530

Dear Mr. Horowitz:

The Federal Bureau of Investigation (FBI) appreciates the opportunity to review and respond to your office's report entitled, *Audit of the Federal Bureau of Investigation's and the National Security Division's Efforts to Coordinate and Address Terrorist Financing* (hereinafter, "Report").

We are pleased you found, "the FBI and NSD have mechanisms to ensure terrorist financing-related information is shared and coordinated with each other and with other law enforcement organizations and intelligence agencies." As noted, "these coordination efforts increase terrorist finance training, supports communication between agencies, and designate organizations who seek to commit or support terrorist acts."

The FBI continues to evaluate and strategize on ways to improve the mission of the Terrorist Financing Operations Section (TFOS). As briefly mentioned in the Report, the FBI restructured TFOS beginning in December 2010. Since that time, FBI efforts to exploit financial intelligence information has increased far beyond your case sampling, which examined counterterrorism cases between fiscal years 2006 through 2010.

In conclusion, we concur with your eight recommendations. Please find enclosed our responses. Should you have any questions, feel free to contact me.

Sincerely,

Andrew G. McCabe
Assistant Director
Counterterrorism Division

Enclosures (2)

**FBI RESPONSES TO THE OIG RECOMMENDATIONS RE
THE FEDERAL BUREAU OF INVESTIGATION'S AND THE
NATIONAL SECURITY DIVISION'S EFFORTS TO COORDINATE
AND ADDRESS TERRORIST FINANCING**

Recommendation 1: Ensure Special Agents appropriately document their use of all financial-related investigative techniques for all counterterrorism investigations.

FBI Response: Concur - The FBI's Counterterrorism Division (CTD), Terrorist Financing Operations Section (TFOS), will provide updated guidance to Special Agents, Intelligence Analysts, Forensic Accountants and Task Force Officers on the appropriate use and documentation of financial-related investigative techniques for counterterrorism investigations.

Recommendation 2: Consider requiring Special Agents to document the valid reasons for not using the six basic financial-related investigative techniques for all counterterrorism investigations.

FBI Response: Concur - Updated guidance will be provided by TFOS to Special Agents, Intelligence Analysts, Forensic Accountants and Task Force Officers regarding the use and documentation of financial-related techniques. The guidance will balance investigative necessity, program management requirements, and administrative burden.

Recommendation 3: Ensure Special Agents adhere to the requirement for the creation of the mandatory financial investigative sub-file for all counterterrorism investigations.

FBI Response: Concur - As per Section 4.8 of the CTD Policy Implementation Guide, the TERRFIN subfile is mandatory in any CT investigation when investigators receive terrorism financing intelligence on the subject or conduct investigative activities regarding the subject's financial background. This subfile must be used to maintain financial records and documents generated as a result of any financial analysis or intelligence collected on a subject's financial activities. TFOS will monitor counterterrorism investigations to ensure compliance with the stated policy.

Recommendation 4: Ensure that Special Agents in the field offices with responsibility for counterterrorism investigations receive on-going training regarding financial-related investigative techniques.

FBI Response: Concur - In coordination with the Training Division, CTD and TFOS will ensure Special Agents, Intelligence Analysts, Forensic Accountants and Task Force Officers receive information and guidance on the use of financial-related investigative techniques.

Recommendation 5: Clearly define the roles, responsibilities, and expectations of the Terrorist Financing Coordinators.

FBI Response: Concur – TFOS is in the process of assessing the Terrorist Financing Coordinator (TFC) duties and responsibilities as the position was originally established 11 years ago prior to TFOS assuming case management responsibilities. Upon completion of the review of the position, TFOS will provide updated guidance regarding the TFC position to the field. To streamline and better coordinate terrorist financing cases, consideration is being given to eliminating the position.

Recommendation 6: Develop, implement, and document formal methods to evaluate the Terrorist Financing Coordinator Conference and other training provided to Coordinators.

FBI Response: Concur - As indicated above in response to #5, TFOS is assessing the current duties and responsibilities of the TFCs.

Recommendation 7: Ensure that there are appropriate written qualifications and training for the field offices' selection of a Terrorist Financing Coordinator as defined by TFOS.

FBI Response: Concur - As indicated above in response to #5, TFOS is assessing the current duties and responsibilities of the TFCs.

Recommendation 8: Ensure that management develops a consistent approach for field offices to include financial-related focus and organization for all counterterrorism investigations.

FBI Response: Concur - Through the FBI's CTD program management efforts, TFOS will continue to provide guidance, instruction and assistance in identifying and utilizing financial intelligence information in counterterrorism investigations. Following the focus and realignment of TFOS in 2011 to an operational section, CTD saw an increase in the awareness and utility of financial intelligence in all types of counterterrorism investigations. For example, relevant financial information is proactively pushed out to investigators on a regular basis, a significant improvement over the previous standard of pulling financial data reactively to support investigative efforts. Active program management of terrorism financing and threat cases is conducted in a coordinated fashion between CTD/TFOS, field offices, Joint Terrorism Task Forces, and Intelligence Community partners. Performance measures are in place for TFOS personnel to ensure that the appropriate level of program management and oversight is conducted.

OFFICE OF THE INSPECTOR GENERAL ANALYSIS AND SUMMARY OF ACTIONS NECESSARY TO CLOSE THE REPORT

The OIG provided a draft of this audit report to the FBI and NSD. The FBI's response is incorporated in Appendix VI of this report. NSD did not provide a formal response but did provide technical comments that are incorporated into the body of this report. The following provides the OIG' analysis of the response and summary of actions necessary to close the report.

Recommendation Number:

1. **Resolved**. The FBI concurred with our recommendation to ensure Special Agents appropriately document their use of all financial-related investigative techniques for all counterterrorism investigations. The FBI stated in its response that the Terrorist Financing Operations Section (TFOS) will provide updated guidance to Special Agents, Intelligence Analysts, Forensic Accountants and Task Force Officers on the appropriate use and documentation of financial-related investigative techniques for counterterrorism investigations.

   This recommendation can be closed when we receive documentation of the updated guidance on the appropriate use and documentation of financial-related investigative techniques.

2. **Resolved**. The FBI concurred with our recommendation to consider requiring Special Agents to document the valid reasons for not using the six basic financial-related investigative techniques for all counterterrorism investigations. The FBI stated in its response that TFOS will provide updated guidance to Special Agents, Intelligence Analysts, Forensic Accountants and Task Force Officers regarding the use and documentation of financial-related techniques, and that the guidance will balance investigative necessity, program management requirements, and administrative burden.

   This recommendation can be closed when we receive documentation of the updated guidance on the appropriate use and documentation of financial-related investigative techniques, including the requirement to document valid reasons for not using the six basic financial-related investigative techniques for all counterterrorism investigations or a written explanation of why such a requirement will not be issued.

3. **Resolved**. The FBI concurred with our recommendation to ensure Special Agents adhere to the requirement for the creation of the mandatory financial investigative sub-file for all counterterrorism investigations. The FBI stated in its response that the sub-file is mandatory in any counterterrorism investigation when investigators receive terrorism financing intelligence on the subject or conduct investigative activities regarding the subject's financial background. The FBI stated that TFOS would monitor counterterrorism investigations to ensure compliance with the stated policy.

This recommendation can be closed when we receive documentation of the procedures in place to ensure compliance with the requirment.

4. **Resolved**. The FBI concurred with our recommendation to ensure that Special Agents in the field offices with responsibility for counterterrorism investigations receive on-going training regarding financial-related investigative techniques. The FBI stated in its response that the Training Division, Counterterrorism Division, and TFOS will ensure Special Agents, Intelligence Analysts, Forensic Accountants and Task Force Officers receive information and guidance on the use of financial-related investigative techniques.

This recommendation can be closed when we receive documentation of the information and guidance on the use of financial-related investigative techniques the Training Division, Counterterrorism Division, and TFOS will provide to Special Agents, Intelligence Analysts, Forensic Accountants and Task Force Officers, as well as a documented timeframe detailing how often this information and guidance will be disseminated.

5. **Resolved**. The FBI concurred with our recommendation to clearly define the roles, responsibilities, and expectations of the Coordinator position. The FBI stated in its response that TFOS is in the process of assessing the Coordinator duties and responsibilities. After the review, TFOS will provide updated guidance regarding the Coordinator position to the field staff. The FBI stated that consideration is being given to eliminating the Coordinator position in an effort to streamline and better coordinate terrorist financing cases.

This recommendation can be closed when we receive documentation of updated guidance clearly defining the roles, responsibilities, and expectations of the Coordinator position to the field or documentation eliminating the position.

6. **Resolved**. The FBI concurred with our recommendation to develop, implement, and document formal methods to evaluate the Terrorist Financing Coordinator Conference and other training provided to Coordinators. The FBI stated in its response that TFOS is assessing the current duties and responsibilities of the Coordinators and will provide updated guidance regarding the Coordinator position to the field.

This recommendation can be closed when we receive documentation of updated guidance on formal methods to evaluate the Terrorist Financing Coordinator Conference and other training provided to Coordinators or documentation eliminating the position.

7. **Resolved**. The FBI concurred with our recommendation to ensure that there are appropriate written qualifications and training for the field offices' selection of a Coordinator as defined by TFOS. The FBI stated in its response that TFOS is assessing the current duties and responsibilities of the Coordinators and will provide updated guidance regarding the Coordinator position to the field.

This recommendation can be closed when we receive documentation of updated guidance on appropriate written qualifications and training for the field offices' selection of a Coordinator or documentation eliminating the position.

8. **Resolved**. The FBI concurred with our recommendation to ensure that management develops a consistent approach for field offices to include financial-related focus and organization for all counterterrorism investigations. The FBI stated in its response that TFOS will continue to provide guidance, instruction, and assistance in identifying and utilizing financial intelligence information in counterterrorism investigations. The FBI also stated that the Counterterrorism Division (CTD) saw an increase in the awareness and utility of financial information in all types of counterterrorism investigations following the focus and realignment of TFOS in 2011. The FBI stated in its response that active program management is conducted in a coordinated fashion between CTD/TFOS, field offices, Joint Terrorism Task Forces, and Intelligence Community partners and that performance measures are in place for TFOS personnel to ensure that the appropriate level of program management and oversight is conducted.

This recommendation can be closed when we receive: (1) documentation of polices in place to ensure that TFOS will continue to provide guidance, instruction, and assistance in identifying and utilizing financial intelligence information in counterterrorism investigations; (2) evidence of the increase in awareness and utility of financial intelligence in all types of counterterrorism investigations; (3) evidence of active program management conducted in a coordinated fashion between CTD/TFOS, field offices, Joint Terrorism Task Forces, and Intelligence Community partners; and (4) documentation of performance measures in place to ensure TFOS personnel conduct an appropriate level of program management and oversight.

www.ingramcontent.com/pod-product-compliance
Lightning Source LLC
Chambersburg PA
CBHW081329310526
45789CB00018B/2707